Julia Peters-Parmeter

FORGOTTEN MEN and WOMEN

Voting to save the American Dream

STRATTON
—PRESS—
Publishing Life

Stratton Press Publishing
831 N Tatnall Street Suite M #188,
Wilmington, DE 19801
www.stratton-press.com
1-888-323-7009

ISBN (Paperback): 978-1-64895-259-3
ISBN (Hardback): 978-1-64895-261-6
ISBN (Ebook): 978-1-64895-260-9

Printed in the United States of America

This book is dedicated to the women who have inspired me to cherish our God, family, and country, above all else!

My mother, Helen Burris, my stepmother Barbara Peters, and two of my best friends, Joan Gatley and Twila LePage-Hughes!

In honor of the forgotten men and women of America!

CONTENTS

A NOTE FROM THE AUTHOR

Dear Reader,

As a first-time author, I am truly humbled that you would choose to read my words. They are not fancy or grammatically perfect, instead they are simple and heartfelt. I am not a scholarly expert, but someone who has been researching as a student for the past decade. My passion for my studies was driven by a desire to heal the nation from what was looking like an upcoming cultural war.

In November 2016, when I heard a persuasive spirit in my conscience telling me to start this book, I argued back with all my doubts and insecurities. And because of my lengthy delays, throughout the past four years, this book has sat on the shelf more than it has been a work in progress. As the manuscript grew from a few pages to a few chapters, I still struggled with little confidence. Until about four months ago, when I found my "Suddenly!"

Suddenly, I knew I needed to finish the project. Suddenly, I knew I just needed to speak from my heart. Suddenly, I did not care if it was not perfect, I did not know what I was doing, or even that my reputation might be trashed. Suddenly, I knew there was a reason that this book sat on the shelf for so long. Suddenly, I realized what I had known before was only a dim view of my impending bold awaking. Suddenly, I knew everything we are experiencing goes much deeper and is much more dire. Suddenly, I knew my timing might not be someone else's. Suddenly, I knew the timing was critical. Suddenly, I knew that "We the People" must get actively involved to save our beloved America and patriots of other countries around the world should follow our lead, or we all run the risk of losing our freedom forever.

Suddenly, I became *feisty*! While I will not apologize for my love of my country, I will apologize for my fearless and passionate dialogue, which gets a little feisty and blatantly honest at times. Because suddenly, I knew that I just could not hold back!

I hope you enjoy reading these pages. Please know I do not expect you to agree with me, though my dialogue may seem persuasive. It is my hope that you develop your own ideas, examine your own thoughts, and challenge your past preconceptions to garner a full awareness of your true feelings.

We all should feel blessed by the constitutional rights and freedoms that we have been given in these United States. Let us exercise them while we can!

May God bless you! And may God bless America!

With love,

Julia

INTRODUCTION

The forgotten men and women of America have made themselves known after many decades of being ignored. These people are the hardworking middle-class patriots who represent the heart of their nation. Although many intellectuals and powerful people have not learned the lessons of the past few years and continue to disregard these forgotten men and women, these forgotten citizens have the ability to save the American Dream by standing up for unity and truth.

It has become increasingly clear that our nation is hugely divided for reasons that everyday citizens cannot comprehend. We have seen this division gradually unfold before our eyes over the past few decades. And now, it has become more apparent than ever. I believe this divide is intentionally perpetrated by some politicians who would like to secure your vote. However, everyday Americans have taken a stand, and they are fighting for the principles in which this country was founded.

This is not a book intended to sway your ideology or beliefs, this book is designed to give you the ability for free thinking and clear expression without the stress misrepresentation or cloud of misinterpretation and to help you gain a clarity to discern. I hate to place blame because that may only promote a greater division, so I will try my best to keep my opinions separate from any facts. However, for those of us who want to mend fences, we do need to examine those manipulators of the truth while making sure that we do not unwittingly become one of them. This book is meant to create an awareness of the current shrewd political tactics that are dividing us as a nation and to offer solutions which will end the ongoing animosities between Americans.

For those of you who want to see an end to this turmoil, which is across our country, I challenge you to participate in searching out the truth, creating an awareness in ourselves as well as others, and working diligently to promote unity in our great nation. You may be one of those who does not want to speak up; however, you may choose to be involved in other ways. You might want to help in a small capacity or you may want to take a larger step in this cause. Just becoming aware might be your goal. Whatever your role in this ministry, uniting our people and bringing about peace and harmony will be our reward. As you determine your level of participation, I will give you some questions to ponder throughout this book. These questions are meant to give you a clear awareness of your potential as a mentor to those you might reach out to in the future and a keen consciousness of the political and cultural environment. Please take the opportunity to write down your answers, so you will have a reference as we progress throughout this book toward our goals. However, whether you choose to become active on some level or not at all, I'm hoping this book will help you recognize political mischief and social injustices that have contributed to the current divisions among our citizens, and I'll encourage you to avoid being blinded by them.

This is *not* a book for Conservatives against Liberals nor is it penned for Republicans against Democrats. Rather, this book takes a stand against the power-driven politicians on both sides of the aisle and the corrupted mainstream media outlets that serve them. Those deceivers are dividing "We the People" intentionally, and "We the People" are the only ones who can stop them. With that said, it is important that I confess to being a Conservative Christian woman who holds opinions regarding political stances, and much of this book will have examples of my experiences being on that side of the political aisle. However, throughout this book, I plan to be as upfront as possible regarding my ideology so that I will not become like those persons that I am about to preach and warn you against. Those persons are not transparent! They are clever prevaricators that represent themselves as fair and balanced while drawing you into their fold. My intention is not to sway you from your true feelings or beliefs; instead, my hope is that you find your own authentic voice.

Let us combine our own individual talents and energies to understand and to help heal and mend the divisions among our people. If you love your country, freedom, and liberty and want to keep it, you are a patriot! Regardless of your race, gender, or creed, it is time for us to simply be Americans. And we can use that unifying label of Americans to bond together because of our common goals for the well-being of our nation and her people.

Let us begin by looking back at the cause of America's divide and then examine how we can move forward to become unified. Let us try to understand each other's political positions, so we can find healthy balances that appeal to the majority and strive for the well-being of all citizens, even the minority. We have more in common than we realize, so let us recognize our similarities and make them known. It is time to salvage our government, as the republic that it was designed to be, a country "of and for the people." We can make the difference for the peace and prosperity of ourselves, our children, and our grandchildren by fighting to restore the American Dream!

CHAPTER 1

America the Beautiful

God shed His grace on thee.
—Katharine Lee Bates in 1895

From sea to shining sea, across this stunning nation, is a land of majestic mountains, wide spreading plains, spectacular lakes and rivers, lush forests, and rich soil. "We the People" of America have been blessed to be able to share this beautiful land and the freedoms, rights, and endless opportunities that come with it. An exceptional country wherein was formed by a few men to leave as a gift to their children and children's children for the prosperity and security of their family's futures. While establishing their own government to be ruled "of and by the people" with liberty and justice for all, America became a desired place to live. Within a short time, this nation became a melting pot for immigrants throughout the world who came to assimilate into America's culture. While seeking a place where they could share common values and work toward a better way of life, they enjoyed an individual right to pursue happiness without infringing on the happiness of others.

Our Founding Fathers created America for one reason, and that was to prevent tyranny. These men turned away from the monarchy of England to create a republic in which they all could take a part. Each citizen claiming a stake and having a vested interest in something they could build and call their own. Settlers found homesteads and worked with their neighbors to build functional communities. Developing a commonwealth with the efforts of farmers, ranchers, doctors, teachers, tradespeople, and entrepreneurs to unite for the good of their citizens. As a republic, these colonies would send representatives to have a voice for their people to share in the ruling of their entire nation. And yet these territories remained separate and apart to maintain their own individuality.

In 1804, President Thomas Jefferson hired the explorers Lewis and Clark to travel west and report back with their findings on the people, plants, animals, and other features of the region. Their long and carefully organized journey left St. Louis, Missouri, and headed up the Missouri River to encounter Native Americans for the first time. Sacagawea, a Native American woman, joined their expedition to serve as a translator during their journey. Into the unknown, these travelers crossed the Great Plains, to the Rocky Mountains, across the Continental Divide, to the Columbia River where they voyaged through rapids and rough waters to finally reach the Pacific Ocean.

Then eureka! In 1848, California ceded to the United States, and gold was discovered by James Marshall in the Sierra foothills along the American River. Leading to the Gold Rush of 1849, when thousands of mostly men headed west by mules, horses, and wagon trains. Soon they would send for their wives and families to settle in the beautiful territories along the West Coast.

It was Presidents Theodore Roosevelt and Woodrow Wilson who looked upon our scenic country and decided to preserve these majestic areas for future generations by designating them as national parks. These magnificent treasures include Yosemite in California, Yellowstone in Wyoming and Montana, Grand Canyon in Arizona, Carlsbad Caverns in New Mexico, Teddy Roosevelt in North Dakota, Mount Rushmore in South Dakota, Glacier and Denali in Alaska, to name a few of the national parks throughout the west. Thus, proving America to be a spectacular destination for tourists who wished to view some of the most scenic places in the entire world.

This is not to say, everything came easy for these founders, settlers, and their families. Quite the opposite is true! Hardship and struggles followed them along the way. There had been tears and pain, due to the endless wars and bloodshed. As years passed, the suffering made us learn and grow as a nation. The ups and downs of strengths and weaknesses have followed America throughout her history, as it has with all nations. However, as a nation formed by the faith-based principles of our founders, we knew that we would always be a humble people before our God, relying on Him to get us through.

In November 1772, John Adams's words in *The Rights of the Colonists* were penned to give evidence of the importance linking our faith to our fundamental rights and freedoms when he wrote, "If men through fear, fraud or mistake, should in terms renounce and give up any essential natural right, the eternal law of reason and the great end of society, would absolutely vacate such renunciation: the right to freedom being a gift of God Almighty, it is not the power of Man to alienate this gift, and voluntarily become a slave."

The American Dream

Truly, the notion of the American Dream began at our country's conception. It was the hopes and promises of our Founding Fathers. However, the term "American Dream" may have first come from author and historian James Truslow Adams in 1931 when he wrote the book *Epic of America*. He spoke of "that dream of a land in which life should be better and richer and fuller for everyone, with opportunity for each according to ability or achievement." Throughout our history, the dream has blossomed with more benefits. We may include Martin Luther King's magnificent words in his "I Have a Dream" speech, in 1963, when he spoke of equality and unity.

The meaning of the American Dream has been elaborated on in a variety of ways, over the years. Those ideas may include many diverse opinions. Some obvious thoughts mention our individual rights and freedoms, which are given to us in our beloved Constitution and Bill of Rights. Our Declaration of Independence, written by Thomas Jefferson, states, "We hold these truths to be self-evident, that all men are created equal, that they are endowed by their Creator with certain unalienable Rights, that among these are Life, Liberty and the pursuit of Happiness." It serves as our mission statement, which offers up the possibilities for the citizens of our country to become whoever and whatever we choose to, regardless of our circumstances at birth. To be able to dream, set goals, and earn success through the opportunities our nation has to offer.

Financially speaking, the American Dream has much to do with our ability to climb the ladder of success. To know that the harder you work, the more you will have. That once you have earned something, it becomes yours, and it cannot be taken away from you. Being a property owner and claiming all rights to that land is a crucial part of our American Dream. This economic component of the Dream tells us that no matter the station in life to which we were born, we too can fulfill our dreams of upward mobility. One of our Founding Fathers, Thomas Jefferson, was influenced by John Locke, whom he considered to be a brilliant philosopher during the Enlightenment Era. Jefferson called Locke "one of the three greatest men the world ever produced."

John Locke penned, "Man...hath by nature a power...to preserve his property—that is, his life, liberty, and estate—against the injuries and attempts of other men." He claimed personal property to be one of his three greatest unalienable rights.

Another admirable element of the American Dream includes "Liberty and Justice for all," which is highlighted in our Pledge of Allegiance, reiterating our constitutional guarantee of the right to due process. This promises us that when we behave in accordance with the laws of our nation, our freedoms and rights are protected. "Justice for all" ensures that both the accused and the victim will get a fair trial by a group of their peers. America's statue of Lady Justice is blindfolded to remind us of the promises of equal treatment under the law, regardless of our race, gender, or creed. Written above the main entrance to our nation's Supreme Court Building appears their motto, which is "Equal Justice under Law," and at the eastern entrance bears the motto "Justice, the Guardian of Liberty." There is no greater gift than our country's legal principle, the "presumption of innocence," which offers the fair protection that one is considered innocent until proven guilty.

In 1863, President Abraham Lincoln delivered the Gettysburg Address, in which his words described America as a nation "conceived in Liberty, and dedicated to the proposition that all men are created equal" and went further to say that "this nation, under God, shall have a new birth of freedom and that government of the people, by the people, for the people, shall not perish from the earth." These powerful words have pointed to one of the most important attributes of our American heritage. No man or woman is to be thought of as more significant than the other, and those individuals have inherited the ability to control their future by participating in the way our country is managed. These values and principles allow diverse citizens across our great land to pick and choose their leaders, who will in turn govern as directed by the will of their constituency.

The Declaration of Independence also proclaims, "That to secure these rights, Governments are instituted among Men, deriving their just powers from the consent of the governed," which is crucial in upholding the freedoms of this nation that belongs to its people. And goes further stating, "That whenever any Form of Government becomes destructive of these ends, it is the Right of the People to alter or to abolish it, and to institute new Government, laying its foundation on such principles and organizing its powers in such form, as to them shall seem most likely to affect their Safety and Happiness." This document is crucial to our republic because it clearly lays out the doctrine which birthed the founding of our nation and gave control to her people.

These appealing factors of the American Dream enticed immigrants from around the world to travel to our incredible nation, with a desire to assimilate into our culture, so that they could pursue their own dreams. Our country soon became a fusion of different nationalities, ethnicities, and cultures, making America a melting pot of diversity. Although those immigrants were multicultural, they were bound together as people who had chosen to become Americans and live the American way of life. Together, with those who had been born in the USA, they created a tapestry of beautiful colors and images, and they gained their strength because of the balance of the diverse talents and gifts they shared with one another. The desire to assimilate as Americans is crucial to unite us as one people who love the one nation of their citizenry. This patriotism is meant to be honorable and not intended to devalue or disrespect any other nations or cultures from which an immigrant may have been born. Eventually, this multiculturalism contributed to making the United States the greatest country on earth and the envy of the entire world.

Currently, most of our poorest citizens live a better quality of life than those in third world countries. (On a separate topic, we will address the homeless crisis in an upcoming chapter.) Middle class Americans have enjoyed proper educations, comfortable lifestyles, and plenty of advantages. And our wealthiest people live like the royalty of other countries. Sadly, many of the beautiful qualities the nation in which we live has to offer have been taken for granted. Some of us may have been blissfully unaware of the huge benefits of this exceptional country, and we never could have imagined that we may run the risk of losing those benefits. I am thinking that I might have been one of those people.

Simply keeping to the facts there is no disputing that although our country has made tremendous blunders, it is a land of great opportunities. I grew up in a middle-class family, and we were given some wonderful advantages. Our grandparents and parents worked hard to afford us those advantages, and we were taught a strong work ethic by the examples of the lives they lived. As my siblings and I became teenagers, we learned to work part-time jobs while going to school, to buy our own clothes, supplies, and vehicles. Earning and setting goals were part of our everyday life, with the vision that we could build our future and pursue our dreams. I never assumed that our country might change one day. I loved our country, and I still do. However, I never realized how much I loved our country until I feared that we might lose it. It is *our* country, and I feel a great sense of territorialism and patriotism in defending America. In this country, "We the People" have been given a huge gift as citizens, the opportunity to express our ideas, use our voice, and exert the right to vote our conscience. This ability to participate in the goodwill of our nation opens the doors that inspire us and our fellow Americans to dream big and strive for more. And best of all, if we fail to attain our dream, we can start over or change our dream. That is the American Dream, and that is what makes America *beautiful!*

For Thoughtful Consideration

Since our nation is filled with citizens of such a variety of circumstances, we all most likely differ in our ideas about the American Dream. Do you think the American Dream means different things to different people? Do you think some people cherish the American Dream more than others? Or do you think some people have just lost sight of the American Dream?

In today's day and age, it seems to me, our children are being taught that if you aspire to attain the American Dream, it is a selfish narcissistic goal. Do you agree? Our children are also being taught with a distorted view of our history, which in many cases creates an unfair perception. Do you think teachers should be obligated to stick to factual and unbiased curriculum?

Let us examine the truth about the American Dream throughout this book because it will help us understand each other, have compassion for one another, and ultimately unite.

CHAPTER 2

Forgotten Citizens

The Land of the Free and the Home of the Brave
—Francis Scott Key in 1814

W ho are these forgotten men and women? They are the hardworking people who keep our country operating. Those everyday Americans who make it possible for us to live the lifestyles that we depend on. You know them as farmers, ranchers, and dairymen who make it possible for our families to eat healthy foods. They are builders, handymen, and tradespeople who give us a place to call home. They are mechanics, bus drivers, and cabbies who make sure that we can get around. They are the receptionists who welcome us with a cheerful smile. They are teachers and daycare providers who educate and guide our children and grandchildren. They are the nurses and caregivers who assist our elderly loved ones. They are our favorite waitresses and bartenders who work in our neighborhood diners. They are our local small business owners who rely on our patronage. They collect our garbage and they clean up our messes. They are our firefighters, police, and military officers who keep us and our families safe.

It goes on and on; these people are crucial to our survival as a nation. Let us be honest, they make our lives a whole lot *better*! These everyday people have a strong work ethic and they struggle to see that their children get every opportunity possible. They might need to work two or three jobs just to make ends meet or provide extras for their kids. These forgotten Americans, doing the best they can in an honest and well-meaning fashion, get up every day to make a better way of life for themselves, their families, and their communities. They are not looking for a handout or a free ride, they are just looking for a fair shake.

We are the majority, and we are the heart of our nation. We are the people who are the proudest of this great country that we love. We are among those who see the realities of our flawed nation and choose to love her regardless. We do not want to lose the fundamental principles given to us by our Founding Fathers because we believe they are precious and rare. Some of us are the melting pot of immigrants, who embraced America's culture, fought hard to get here, and worked so rigorously to become United States citizens. We are a family of Americans who would like to believe that all of us, whether natural -born citizens or true immigrants, will respect one another and our nation's great Constitution, laws, and history. Our unconditional love for our country is what binds us together and makes us patriots!

If you fall into the category of middle class, as most of us do, you are busy. You are going along pursuing your right to happiness, minding your own business, following the laws of the land, working hard, and struggling to make ends meet. You might not have much time to notice the daily news and politics that affect you and your family, and quite honestly, most of us probably could care less. Keeping you occupied with endless labor and totally unaware is the plan of those who control the world. The powerful wealthy elitists and dishonest political leaders would prefer you remain oblivious because as this ruling class promote their power-driven agendas, they need to keep you dependent on them. So they continually beat you down with burdensome taxes and strict business regulations that make it impossible for you to get ahead, leading you to a vicious cycle of needing to work more and become more exhausted. These thieves continually take more of your money, then line their pockets from their dirty shenanigans. As these governing leaders corruptly perform malicious backdoor deals to further their wealth, they claim to be giving larger handouts to the less fortunate citizens then boast that they are morally superior to you. This repetitive pattern is what keeps the ruling class in power, as "We the People" become further ignored and blatantly abused. We have been cast down as enslaved forgotten Americans.

The working-class citizens have not only been forgotten and beaten down for the past several decades, they have also been shamed when complaining about any lack of fairness. Here are two interwoven examples of the types of injustices with which the disregarded common people have been forced to deal. The first has always been a pet peeve for me. The everyday folks pay full price for almost everything, while others get a break. Let us take the extremely high college tuitions that we may be expected to spend for our children, while someone else from another country may pay no tuition by being granted government funding. As an American taxpayer, we should not be paying for the education of a citizen from another country. The second injustice involves my point regarding shaming because if we complain about the first injustice, we will be called out as an uncompassionate or reprehensible human being. So as they kick us when we are down, unless we want to be labeled by some slanderous name, we keep quiet and hold our feelings back. The American middle class has lost the ability to express their views openly and without attack unless it suits the political agenda of those in charge. We might as well forget trying to defend ourselves against the inequities and abuse that have led to our being abandoned by these uncaring politicians. This shaming is one of the reasons "We the People" have lost control of the narrative that is driving our land. However now, because of these injustices and endless others like them, we can see that they are not keeping their pretty campaign promises. So we become aware that they only have contempt for us. We are being used as political tools in their deceptive games, simply to score our votes.

Forgotten Americans are not your snobby elites, which include politicians, business tycoons, famous Hollywood stars, and legendary athletes. A great majority of this affluent elitist group have birthed a generation of entitled brats, who cannot cope with the realities of their lives and choose to be spiritually weak and emotionally immature. Much of this wealthy 1 percent of our population have become addicted to their fame and fortune, and they simultaneously corrupted their perspective on reality and any conscientiousness of their spirituality. While promoting an agenda that maintains their social status, these self-absorbed elites are sucking the fun out of everything. Unfortunately, I believe many in this group have been responsible for misguiding the public and stoking their confusion, which has led to the problems we are currently facing of divisions within our nation. Though they mock us, we the forgotten men and women have elevated these elites to their proverbial thrones, and now we must reject them, once and for all. We will soon dig deeper into some strategies that will break the control these powerful elites have over us, the everyday Americans.

In the upcoming chapters of this book, I want to also show you how many of our forgotten men and women have become the true national superheroes of this current cultural drama that has been unfolding in America. And how they have set a positive patriotic example to other countries around the world. By becoming inspirational freedom fighters throughout our country, we have joined one another in a movement to benefit this whole nation. Our battle has not been one provoked because of racism, bigotry, gender phobia, or any other kind of phobia. In fact, it has not been mean-spirited in any way. Our goal has been to reclaim our sovereign rights and hand the controlling power of our government back to its people, both have been slipping away from us for decades. And though some of our battles have been won, the war certainly is not over. So for all of us patriots who would like to save the United States of America for the future generations of our children and grandchildren, it is time to strongly hold our ground and bravely protect our precious nation, by standing up for our precious values of "truth, liberty, justice, and the American way."

FORGOTTEN CITIZENS

The Far Left or the Far Right

Regardless of your political party, you might have become a forgotten American. It is important to remember this fact throughout the course of this book, the term of forgotten American does not only apply to one specific group of people; it is not based on their ethnic, religious, gender, or political identity. It describes many citizens of these United States who simply were not being taken care of and their voices were being ignored. However, keep in mind, though they are the victims of a current raging political war, these forgotten Americans do not act like victims; they have been brave, resilient, and strong. These crusaders have managed to get through one crucial battle after another in their pursuit to maintain control of their nation. They had been deeply let down by the two decades of governmental administrations. And it was the elite establishment politicians of both parties, Republican and Democrat, who had abused and neglected them.

Most Americans are neither of the Far Left or the Far Right, in fact, the majority hover directly in the middle. Liberals and Conservatives are not as polarized as we have been told, but unfortunately, many people do not realize this. There is no reason for us to be at each other's throats, and if you hang with me throughout this book, I will continually confirm this statement. When we focus on the common ground between us, we will overcome the fragmented society that has been thrust upon us. In this current moment, it is important that those who have wished to remain neutral to the ever-mounting political struggles briefly come out of the fog to realize that their American Dream is at stake. This is not a time to be blissfully unaware or complacent. This ensuing cultural war, as the result of political manipulation to garner your vote, is ultimately intended to cease your rights and freedoms. "We the People" are not each other's enemy, we are on the same team. Power-mongering elitists, who wish to divide and overtake us, are our enemy. They have enslaved us! But before we go into that, we must reflect on some of the things from our history that have ripened the playfield to create the separations within our people and have ultimately driven us further and further apart.

The history of America's roots is filled with dramatic events that have led us to become the nation that we are today. All countries are filled with sinful stains that tarnish their fabric and, like the United States, have overcome with the blood and suffering of both good and bad men. Those roots are blemished; however, they are also a foundation that we cherish as a nation based on our common beliefs, rights, privileges, and dreams. The dramatic events of the past, which have brought our land stress and turmoil, are the originators of both positive unity and detrimental division, the first, which was intended to lead to a peaceful coexistence, and the second, which was perpetrated by those with a lust for power and greed. One step toward our solidarity as a nation will be recognizing the prior patterns that led to harmony, and then using them as a road map to our future. But unless we learn from our past mistakes and make the necessary changes, we will never obtain the place of well-being that we desire. We must pay attention to those previous errors and learn from them or else we may be doomed to repeat them endlessly.

Our first President George Washington was inaugurated on April 30, 1789. He appointed Alexander Hamilton to be Secretary of the Treasury and Thomas Jefferson as Secretary of State. These men were part of a group that Washington convened regularly, soon to be known as his Cabinet. Unfortunately, Hamilton and Jefferson disagreed on almost every issue. In the early 1790s, two political parties started to form. These organized groups became known as factions. President Washington was not pleased with the factions; he warned that these divisions would destroy the "best fabric of human government and happiness."

As we have watched our history unfold, we have witnessed that sadly, Washington's words were a foreshadowing of what was to come. "We the People" have been the victims of these factions, and we have discovered just how dangerous they are to our ability to maintain unity between our citizens. To bring the American people together, we should reverse this separation, end these political divisions, and become a one-party republic once again. The majority of

Americans are divided because of the misconceptions they have been given about one another. Most of us tend to be politically moderate, possibly leaning a bit to the right or the left.

Eventually, the two political parties became known as Republicans and Federalists. The Republicans argued that the federal government was growing too strong under President Washington. They wanted to keep most of the power with the people because they feared that a federal government with too much strength would ultimately act like a monarchy. Whereas, the Federalists felt that the strong government should be led by wealthy and educated men who would be in control of the states and townships. Another clear difference between the parties is that the Republicans opposed high tariffs, a tax on imported goods, while the Federalists favored these taxes. Also, the Federalists under Hamilton supported a nation bank and Jefferson's Republicans opposed the federal bank. Among their differences, Republicans sought a strict interpretation of the Constitution, and the Federalists preferred a loose interpretation.

Although the Federalist Party in the 1850s became the Democrat Party, the fundamental principles of both parties have not changed too much over the past two centuries. The disputes between these two parties have been ongoing throughout our American history. There have even been divisions within the parties themselves. An early example was during the presidential election of 1860. Abraham Lincoln represented the Republican Party. However, the Democrat Party was divided with a Northern and a Southern Democrat candidate, which led to Lincoln's victory. In 1861, disagreements over slavery led to the Civil War between the Republican Union Army of the North and the Democrat Confederate Army of the South. And in 1863, President Lincoln's Emancipation Proclamation ended slavery and opened the way for the African Americans to join the Conservative Union army. Under the leadership of Ulysses S. Grant, the Union Army won the Civil War in April 1865, and the African American people gained their freedom with an end of slavery. Lincoln not only managed to save the Union, but he also become a hero to the North and the African American people of this nation. John Wilkes Booth, who was a Confederate sympathizer that lamented the abolition of slavery, assassinated President Lincoln on April 14, 1865.

Before we move forward, I must be clear that while I will be using the term Liberal or Democrat, I do not believe that all Liberals and Democrats are the same. Just as not all Conservatives and Republicans are the same. We all are individuals with different degrees of separation within our ideologies and parties. It is the extreme Leftists and the extreme Right-Wing that tend to get us in turmoil and heated debates. Most of my comments about Liberals will refer to the radical far left wing of the Democrat Party, and that group often tends to be a minority within their mix; however, they can be the most vocal, have the loudest voices, and be portrayers of the greatest extreme acts. This Leftist group leans toward Marxism and Communist views.

Many people who choose to be a Liberal, do so because they believe Liberalism is a more compassionate and generous ideology. That is why for years they were regarded as Bleeding Heart Liberals. Those caring and kind Liberals see themselves literally, as the word Liberal is defined to be.

Webster's Dictionary defines *Liberal* as an adjective meaning, [[< L liber, free]] 1. Generous 2. Ample; abundant 3. Not literal or strict 4. Tolerant; broadminded 5. Favoring reform or progress. As a noun meaning, 1. One who favors reform or progress.

On the surface, the basic concepts of the term Liberal are the admirable qualities of a well-meaning person. From a political standpoint, those qualities are still respectable, unless they are used inappropriately. And the exact same can be said of those who are Conservatives.

Webster's Dictionary defines Conservative as an adjective meaning, 1. Tending to conserve 2. Tending to preserve established institutions, etc.; opposed to change 3. Moderate; cautious As a noun meaning, 1. A conservative person.

The most basic differences between modern-day Democrats and Republicans can be evident in their definitions. Democrats are for big government and Republicans are for small government. Democrats are for more taxes and Republicans are for less taxes. Democrats are for more spending and Republicans are for less spending. Democrats are looser with the Constitution and its laws and Republicans are stricter. Democrats are for change and Republicans are for keeping the founding standards. While Democrats claim to be Civil Rights Advocates, our US history proves the Republican Party to be the Civil Rights Warriors. However, with all those facts, it may very well be that the social issues of which each party take a stance have become the most divisive elements between them. Although keep in mind, there are many political party members who choose to support the stances of their opposing political party. For one example, you can have many Pro-Life Democrats or Pro-Choice Republicans. Which brings me back to the fact that none of us should be judged by the political choices that we make. It is somewhat like, not judging a book by its cover.

*****

This is a great time to be alive! Forgotten men and women have stepped up to regain their independence and power. They are becoming more aware every day of the "bag of goods that they were being sold." Collective voices are rising, not just for themselves, but for their fellow citizens. Today's politics is no longer boring; this has become a defining moment for the United States. "We the People," who are the forgotten men and women, must vote again to save our American Dream!

For Thoughtful Consideration

Forgotten Americans have been overlooked by our society in general. Have you recognized that they have become an ignore group? Do you feel that they can take care of themselves, thus they do not need to be considered in the decisions that affect our nation? Do you feel that America is still a country "of and for the people?"

Today, it appears as if the mention of your political party is met with an assumption of certain character traits of a person affiliated with that certain group. Do you feel reluctant to say which party that you are a member of for this reason? Do you stigmatize others, with a personal view of them, based on their political party? If so, which personal judgments stand out in your mind?

CHAPTER 3

Our Free-Thinking Culture

*Preservation of one's own culture does not require
contempt or disrespect for other cultures.*

—Cesar Chavez

B eing founded as a nation "of and for the people" should mean
that our citizens will determine the structure of our cultural
foundation. However, a culture can easily be manipulated
within its boundaries because of some primary groups of social influencers. We can only hope that those who exert the power to sway
the people within our land can be trusted with our best interests at
heart. They can affect the minds and behaviors of all of us in very
dramatic ways, based on the authority they are given in the places of
significance within our lives.

In order to be a freethinker, we must avoid the traps set out for
us, in the most persuasive regions of our life. There are so many triggers, some subliminal and others obvious, that can affect our mood,
thoughts, and behaviors. It would be rare that any of us could say
that we hold organic biased opinions. We all have spent our life's
journey experiencing, growing, challenging, and educating ourselves. We have been given extraordinary opportunities, freedoms,
and blessings in America. Our choices lead us in targeted directions,
but it is of whom we choose to listen, where we place their credibil-

ity, and how much importance they have in our development as a human being. The best way to be a freethinker is to be aware of the cognitive power those around us can exert over our minds and be determined to examine any motive behind their message. Most of the time, a motive can be purely for our benefit and void of any ill intent. Finding trusted mentors throughout your life is a true blessing.

The forgotten men and women have not been in a position of influence. We have been the victims of our society by a group of self-designated superior-minded bullies. These intimidators have undermined our intelligence, and they will chastise any of us who disagree with them. They deem us worthless and beneath them. We, the forgotten ones, have had no control of the narrative guiding our culture for the past several decades. Therefore, as we are rendered voiceless and unimportant, we struggle to find a place of relevancy within our borders. However, we can choose not to be their passive victims and counter their false narratives by becoming aware and awakening others.

Some of the most influential areas of society which impact people and civilizations are religion, social groups, government, business, academia, media, arts, entertainment and family. Many of the "woke" members of our world are becoming aware of the infiltration of these areas with influencers who hope to control our thoughts and actions by convincing us that their ways are superior to others, thus creating and molding us to a society under their emotional grasp. While we think we are making our own decisions, we are making our choices based on the formed opinions of these persuaders. Being aware of the tricks of those who are obvious in their deception is the best way to avoid being the victim of disinformation or biased propaganda.

Let us examine each area of influence that touches our lives and makes us the ideological people we choose to become. We develop our character by the circumstances that we let affect our nature. Journaling your thoughts as you are reading throughout this chapter may help you understand yourself and how you perceive others. Keep in mind, understanding ourselves benefits us personally, but also helps us to better understand others. And ultimately guides us to the goal of this book, which is to unite America.

OUR FREE-THINKING CULTURE

Family

Our family influences us daily, starting as early as when we were an infant at birth. Children are taught basic behavior traits from their family members. It is in our earliest years that we develop a knowledge of the difference between good and bad, right and wrong, love and hate, happy and sad. And it is in our early years they we begin to develop our moral compass. Our personalities grow based on our circumstances and level of self-esteem. If we admire one family member more than another, we may develop that family member's philosophies and personality traits. If we fall into the category of a people pleaser, we may make choices for our future accordingly to how we feel our family members will respond. An example may be your father, whom you would never want to let down, has a strong work ethic, so you in turn feel that your personal value will come from working extremely hard. Our families may have customs and traditions that set the foundation for our upbringing that may even be multicultural. These may include the closeness and importance of family or lack thereof. Your religious beliefs can be natured and formed by your family. And the extent and quality of education can be swayed by family. Choices in entertainment, including sports, can also influence us based on participation by members of our family, and so on and so on.

My upbringing forms the opinion, which is weaved together with facts, throughout the pages of this book. I was born on April 2, 1961, in Oakland, California. So my childhood spanned the '60s and early '70s, and I was a teenager in the late '70s. We were a middle-class family. My father was a firefighter and my mother was a stay-at-home mom. I was the first of five children, and we were raised Roman Catholic. Our parents sent us to Catholic elementary schools, where we were taught by Spanish nuns. They could be extremely strict. I witnessed these teachers pulling out many a ruler to hit naughty children, not to mention pull them out of the classroom by their ears. These religious women also instilled in me something called Catholic guilt, along with a firm Christian foundation and a love for God.

I grew up in what I termed the *Brady Bunch* and the *Partridge Family* days. Family shows like *The Waltons* and *Happy Days* were filled with clean living, and they showed us what true family values were all about. Our heroes were fictional characters, like Batman and Robin and Superman and Wonder Woman, who fought against evil, for the sake of truth and justice. Cowboys, like John Wayne, were the good guys that we admired. These role models were brave, compassionate, and always did the right thing. Movies taught us about anti-heroes, too. They were the bad guys that did despicable deeds. Our entertainment industry certainly had an impact on our way of life.

My parents were Republican, and they taught me about politics. I was fortunate to live in California where we had Ronald Reagan as our governor for eight years, from 1967 to 1975, and then to have him as my president for eight years, from 1981 to 1989. I thought Reagan was the ideal politician and so did most Conservatives.

Our family sets the foundation of our lives, and some of us have better circumstances than others. However, none of us should become victims of our circumstances. We must always remember that we live in the land of the American Dream, in which every person can elevate themselves to another economic station in life. And we can enjoy the freedoms our country has to offer by choosing those we admire to influence us throughout life's journey. So although we may love our families, our individuality is developed by the choices we make for our futures.

Church

Church is another major influence in our lives and something that we typically attend with our families from a young age. The traditions and values of our religious life are sure to sway our moral compass. And church is sure to influence us, depending on our level of commitment to our faith and our level of admiration for our religious leaders. These leaders set powerful standards for us to live by. Of course, the Holy Bible, the Koran, and other religious books are sometimes the most influential guidelines for which we choose to shape our lives. And if we lack church or God in our lives, we may base our circumstances and how we view our world in an entirely different way. From a cultural standpoint, the church can be a major influence on how nation is perceived. And because we are a country of diverse religions, this can be an overwhelming prospect if we are not tolerant and respectful of one another. Tolerance and respect are crucial to our understanding of the way we view our neighbor's choice of worship, and it should be considered in making decisions that affect us at a community, state, and national level. In the same way, America being a country founded on Christian principles should not be threatened by those with differing religious ideas. My thought is firm: those who chose to be a part of our nation should be accepting of our love for our God, and yet as a free nation, we citizens should be respectful of others to worship as they please. We look at this opinion further in the upcoming chapter I have titled "Politics and Religion."

For those who do not follow a spiritual path, they too can be touched by churches and the faithful in their communities because there is always an element of religious traditions surrounding holiday seasons. This can affect society in two ways. Firstly, you may have the unfaithful celebrating the spiritual event, simply to enjoy the joyous activities and/or gift-giving process. Those unfaithful ones may think that they should control the narrative though by possibly requesting changes which push God further from the reason for the season. You find those hypocrites, as I put it, "liking the party but forgetting *why* they were invited." And secondly, there is the flip side of the heathens who have often been reluctant to be respectful of any displays of religious symbolism, and as time goes by, you can often see them blatantly disregard religion institutions by their efforts to eliminate any sign of God from our culture. Those forms of influence are meant to breakdown our cultural freedoms.

Academia

The radical activists of the 1960s are now the liberal professors that are teaching our children in universities all over our great nation.

They have gone as far as indoctrinating our youth with their biased political views. While posing as honorable teachers, they have swayed the millennials of our time with their liberal ideology. In some cases, they use grade intimidation as a weapon, creating an impression that a student is somehow smarter or dumber based on their ideology. Many of these professors no longer instruct our youth with facts, instead they alter our American history to suit their political agendas. What is most disturbing is the demonizing of nation that leaves our children with negative images of our country, rather than focusing on the founding principles that make America unique, desirable, and exceptional.

It has become increasingly clear that most modern-day educators do not preach good work ethics or show our children how to cope with the realities in the world outside their campuses. Some of the young adults are coming away from educational institutions book smart but emotionally destroyed. Privileged attitudes, entitled rich kids, angry millennials are leaving some very prestigious universities filled with very radical ideas. As parents, it is wise to look at the instructors and talk to our children to see if their teachers are expressing facts or infusing their opinions throughout lectures. Be wary because it is amazing how early that they start indoctrinating children with persuasive thoughts.

I remember a story that I heard about a young woman coming home from college for spring break and she was quite upset with her father because he was a Conservative. She said, "Dad, don't you know how horrible the greedy Republicans are?"

He ignored her question and asked, "How are you doing in school, honey?"

She replied, "I am getting straight As."

"That's great, sweetheart! How is your friend Suzy doing?"

"Suzy is not getting very good grades, she has a C average. But she is having lots of fun and partying all the time."

Her dad smirked. "Why don't you split your grades with her? You both could have Bs in all your classes."

She gave him a rant. "Dad, you can't do that. And besides, it would not be fair to me. I work hard for those As, and I earned them.

And because I am tired all the time, I don't go to the parties and have any fun. Suzy needs to be more disciplined and work harder if she wants to get better grades."

He winked at his daughter and ended the conversation with "Honey, welcome to the Republican standard. I am afraid to tell you, you are a Conservative."

Entertainment

The entertainment industry has molded our culture throughout the past century. It is crazy to think how far we have come since the roaring 1920s. Music changed rapidly. Films emerged with an overwhelming excitement. Musicians and movie stars were adored and idolized. The performers evolved with the times, and the fans changed by the influence of those celebrities who were the most popular. Like a domino effect, we could see how the entertainment world was touching and changing our nation's lifestyles, especially in the big cities. Over the decades, the world of entertainment has determined our very nature of how we move, behave, look, and dress. We could see it leading us into new eras of social promiscuity. Eventually, forcing us to discern what was morally acceptable and what was not, which soon threatened our likelihood of mutual agreement.

Hollywood has filled our minds with make-believe perceptions of the way life is and how life should be. They also tell us how we should think and how we should feel. It may be subtle, but it is there. Then, as if that does not affect you enough, we run the risk of holding ourselves to what can be an unattainable standard. You see your favorite actors, and they set your standard. However, you only see them when their makeup is perfect, their dialogue is cleverly scripted, and their false reality appears to be out-of-this-world (because it is!). Maybe you wish that your parents could be so awesome. Maybe you hope that your marriage would be that romantic. Or maybe you long for that spotless lifestyle. Excuse me, I do not mean to sound so cynical because we all enjoy losing ourselves in those "happily ever after" genres of entertainment. However, those powerful images can manipulate the way we expect ourselves and our lives to be, and they can set us up for some major disappointments. I have often wonder if those false realities are why divorce rates have skyrocketed, family units have broken down, and drug and alcohol abuse are out of control.

Films and television have also become beacons of what is acceptable. The moral standards in our society have been guided by what we see on the screen. Hollywood pushes the envelope as far as possible in what we will deem satisfactory, and we condone their advancement of more and more disturbing content. Extreme violence and bloodshed lead to more carnage in our world. Film makers need to take responsibility for romanticizing acts of violence which can easily influence their audiences. They are the ones promoting fear, anger, and violence. Yet you hear them blame the guns and our Second Amendment, when we all know the weapon is an inanimate object, with the inability to pick itself up. In some cases, this becomes an intentional ploy with a political agenda. In the same respect, Hollywood also needs to stop promoting hate by demonizing certain groups of people in their projects. Unjustly charactering is used to sway the audience to misjudge others. This can be dangerous and contributes to the deep divisions between members of our society. Boycotting these films is the best answer because they promote some negative and destructive messages. Our dilemma becomes the fact that there is less and less good family entertainment. Family shows are mainly for the very young, and the quality of entertainment has suffered tremendously. So teenagers and adults end up choosing shows which attract us by the actors who are in them, and if you are like me, we watch hesitantly, then cringe and close our eyes throughout many of the disturbing scenes.

Somewhat like peer pressure, I believe most wannabe entertainers form a great deal of their opinions based on the need to fit in with the Hollywood scene. They want to succeed in this incredibly tough business, so they will follow along, no matter what the cost. They wreak of desperation, and their lack of confidence in their ability to succeed by way of their talent makes them grovel and conform to the ideology of those who hold their fate in their hands. And we all know that Hollywood has become a liberal playground, so the weak play the game.

Another factor is that many young actors are star struck themselves, so they are easily swayed by the popular musicians and actors who they admire the most. These talents are prone to wanting to become celebrities for all the wrong reasons. They hold too much importance on the opinion of famous people, who sometimes have very little intelligence for anything other than the material that is written for them.

To be a star name actor, famous musician, or legendary sports star is a great privilege. With that honor, these celebrities should be held to a standard that carries an obligation to respect their fan base. Respect does not mean influencing your fans with your personal ideology and then condemning them when they think differently than yourself. Preying on impressionable young people is a cruel form of manipulation, and it should be challenged and rebuked. Respecting others means giving them a chance to examine their own morals, values, and social stances because all people have different views based on their circumstances, which make up their own perceptions of what is right and what is wrong and what works and does not work.

La-La Land attracts you with the lure of intrigue, conflated hype and glamorous celebrities. They tell you what is popular and what is not popular. They tell you who is cool and who is not cool. As we obliviously enjoy their movies and TV shows, the powers behind the scenes program our minds with intentional messages, some that are presented as obvious to the viewer and some by way of the use of subliminal imagery. Most of us give them the ability to sway us because we do not understand the harmful nature or the long-term consequences of its purpose. Does it sound like I am suggesting a conspiracy theory? Yes, I am! But I hate to jump ahead; we will cover the reasons behind their objectives throughout this entire book. And what I am hinting at is a possible plan to evolve our culture in a way that empowers and enriches the ruling class by beating down the forgotten men and women and weakening the stability of our society, thus making us all dependent on those powerful elite.

FORGOTTEN MEN AND WOMEN

Mainstream News Media

Most people hear and see the news through the mainstream media outlets, never suspecting that they may be swaying you to think a certain way with their biased tones of voice, their very clever use of descriptive words or a tainted manipulation and twisting of actual stories. These purveyors of the important messages can form our opinions, with what they choose for us to hear and see. The most divisive tool in creating the current lack of unity among our American citizens is the mainstream media because they control the way the public is influenced politically and socially on a twenty-four-hour daily basis. They control their audiences with the news stories they choose for us to view and hear and even suppress the ones they wish to withhold to fit their political agendas. Journalists no longer tell their stories in a fair and balanced way. Remember the days of hearing the facts without any biased tones or seeing any judgment in the expressions of the newscasters' faces. If you are under fifty years old, chances are that those days have not been during your lifetime. Most recently, the mind-altering material has gotten out of hand. And the media's biases have been more obvious than ever before. It is particularly troubling for Conservatives when they are represented by only seven news outlets, compared to the Liberal's thirty-two outlets. The other problem for Conservative outlets is that they tend to be honest and present mostly facts, while the Liberal outlets share loads of juicy propaganda and use speculation. You may say that, that is my opinion; however, it can be proven easily to those who wish to acknowledge it. Liberal outlets have been forced to retract so many stories in the past decade, hopeful that you will not see their mistakes. My actual opinion in this matter is that Liberal news outlets intend to be deceitful and sensationalize their narratives in order to win viewership and push their left-wing agenda; however, they are banking on the fact that only some of their audience will hear their retractions.

Regardless, the mainstream news media and even your local news outlets have not been unbiased reporters of the news, as they were fifty years ago. Offering just the facts in their entirety is long gone. These so-called journalists have controlled our thoughts and manipulated our culture for decades, and the result has been damaging to the integrity of our nation and her people.

Social Media and the Internet

Facebook, Twitter, Instagram, YouTube and many more social media platforms are determining what is appropriate and what is not. They control the narrative around the entire world by rejecting material they deem unfit and promoting content with which they wish to guide your thoughts and emotions. Truth has become irrelevant to those controlling the narrative. Unwittingly, you are saturated with the stories that these powerbrokers want you to hear and see, while they suppress the ones that do not suit their agenda. You become a victim of their mind manipulation, so slowly conform to their forced ideology.

When you open your web browser, the home page filled with current news, which can be extremely biased. Yahoo and Comcast are very Liberal and almost always have a negative condescending twist to the Conservative viewpoint.

Google and other information-providing companies have the power to control the search engine as to which material you receive. This has been a masterful tool to create distorted realities that can be manipulated to sway opinion. It has been proven that these entities of the information that we request have the ability, and use it, to give you positive or negative commentaries to affect your thoughts. We witnessed this in a hyper-accentuated way during the 2016 presidential election process. There were fake stories, regarding the candidates and their campaigns, on both sides of the aisle. These untrue stories led to hate, anger, and disgust, causing endless feuds between friends, loved ones, and acquaintances. Several former Google employees have come forward to express their concern over Google's censorship tactics to alter upcoming elections, too. Their Liberal strategy is for Conservative points of view to be taken down and limited from the audience's reach. And they can control the content that the public sees by putting out positive or negative stories about the candidates based on their political party or agenda. Google promotes their Liberal ideology by using praiseworthy positive stories for the Left-Wing candidates, while pushing negative narratives which can damage the Right-Wing candidates.

Also, beware when searching for the truth. The fact checkers are not necessarily always factual. They too have been proven wrong in many instances. So it is best to be very careful when determining the credibility of the material that you receive from the internet.

Business

Some large corporations use powerful pressure to form their lower level workers into a company compliance which can easily lead to their submission of thought. Workers who wish to advance to a higher ranking within the structural system of one's career can be influenced by those who hold the keys to their success. Intimidation is a tool tactic of those in authority, and the reward is usually based on a new level of prestige and financial positioning. Money and greed are great motivators of the stances one takes socially and politically. From the young up-in-comers, who are hoping to climb the ladder of success in the world of finance and economics, to the moguls of Wall Street, we can see the lust for more wealth as their driving force. Rich family dynasties and elite politicians also fall into the category of the "worshipers of the money god." While they make their claims to care for the impoverished by giving large donations, they influence those around them to promote ideologies that contribute to an oppression of the poor. Therefore, we see the rich get richer and the poor get poorer. And the forgotten men and women, who are in the middle, gradually get crushed!

Trade Unions have become radicalized in pushing their union members to vote for Left-Wing politicians and their political agendas. There was a time when the Democrat Party had principles that benefited the working man and woman, but those days seem to be long gone. I have often wondered why these trade unions would support politicians and political agendas that directly hurt the members they claim to represent. I will not be surprised if we soon find out that there have been malicious dealings and/or payoffs going on. Hmmm? We shall see!

Bottom line, vote your conscience!

Social Groups

Peer pressure is a great motivator in the decisions that we make and the people that we become. Choose your friends wisely!

We should all be wary of the groups of people with whom we associate. Trusting those we regard as friends is crucial. And sometimes, acquaintances are best to remain just that. Helping our children by teaching them about the lessons that we all have had to endure is one of the best gifts that we can give them. And then pray that they will listen.

I remember, when we had first been married, telling my husband how much fun I had been having with some of his friends. I had been newer to the area where we were living, and he had lived there his entire life. We were discussing one of my conversations with a few local women, and Tom said, "Be careful!"

I wondered, "Why?"

He warned, "Trust me! Only believe half of what you hear."

Dumbfounded, I questioned him, "Which half?"

He simply replied, "Exactly!"

It may have sounded very sarcastic, and we do spend a great deal of our time teasing one another, but I will never forget the idea behind his message.

In life, we want to believe that everyone we encounter is as loving and kind as hope to be; however, some people may not have our best interests in mind. I will never forget one of my many lessons learned. After school, while our children were playing, there were about five mothers that I was hanging out, almost daily. One of the gals was mad at me, for some unknown reason. I was baffled, what could I have done? In my wildest dreams, I could never imagine that one of the other mothers would make something up, just so she could have her friend all to herself. That was a rude awakening that I truly needed to experience in my life because now I use it to tell my daughters and my loved ones to be wary. Understanding who we can truly trust, in all instances, is a blessing.

We can be influenced in all sorts of ways by the people that we choose to spend our time around. The private clubs we join, the social events we participate in, and the activities that we enjoy with others, all determine the experiences that contribute to the way we think. Our thoughts can be affected by those we admire, and the attitudes we develop are because of the challenges we face in our relationships. Some of the organizations, in which we become involved, can sway us based on our need to fit in socially. Those of us who are strong-willed and have great strength of character are less likely to be impacted by the opinions of others and conform to their approval.

Whom we choose to trust and listen to are very important tasks. When we find trusted sources, listening and researching the facts of the issues that affect our lives is so crucial to our well-being. And being a freethinker means knowing the desires of your own heart and the understanding of your true feelings.

Government

Our United States government and its bureaucratic institutions have been hijacked by greedy politicians, who we have thought of as our representatives, hopeful that they would have America's well-being in mind. "We the People" are supposed to be the decision makers, and our vote is supposed to be the authority. The beauty of being a republic is that the citizens choose the leaders who they think will appropriately follow our Founding Fathers' Constitutional guidelines and the best interests of their American constituency. With our vote, it is our influence that should have been swaying our ruling class; however, the fundamental principles of our governmental system have been twisted to benefit them, with more power and riches. The establishment elite politicians on both sides of the aisle, Republicans and Democrats, are at fault for the destruction of our republic. "We the People" will only regain control of our nation and the privilege of participating in its prosperity if we heighten the public's awareness with our knowledge and understanding.

Their goal is not only to enrich themselves, but to have complete control of our ability to choose. Ironic, right? The Left-Wing hypocrisy is such that, while you can choose to end a life or live in America illegally, you should not be able to choose the school which your child will attend or choose the healthcare plan for your family.

Currently, the Democrat politicians are manipulating our options for voting, which would place voter integrity at risk. And what have we heard about their efforts to make Washington, DC, a state? Wow! That sounds fishy! Changing the rules of the Constitution to suit yourself, by improving your ability to cheat or win an election, is beyond despicable!

So while we can, we all must exercise our right to vote. And vote wisely!

Cultism

Can you imagine a world where we all looked the same, had the same voice, thought the same thoughts, moved the same way, like the same things, and followed the same routines? Yikes! None of that appeals to me. Does it appeal to you? We would not be special, unique, or precious. I am old enough to remember a bizarre film called *The Stepford Wives* from 1975; they did a remake in 2004. Creepy perfect women who were probably some sick men's fantasy partners. These robot-type meticulous housewives are akin to modern-day zombies. Brain dead!

A cult is known as a group of people sharing the same beliefs. The goal of these clan members is the mind control and submission of its people. The cult leaders prey upon innocent weak-willed individuals, who usually are away from their homes. The cult group becomes your family and friends. These sects further isolate their victims by using persuasive measures to lure them away from loved ones by "Love Balming." This deceptive tactic pulls their target into a deeper form of management. They lure you with charming flattery and lovely promises, and they incessantly tell you that they love you. Once you have been roped in, they require you to do the same to new members. They may even require you to recruit new members. And in return, they expect total conformity.

I have had a strange and full life. It amazes me the experiences that I have been through over nearly six decades. One of those teaching moments, in my early twenties, was my time in a religious cult. I can still remember details vividly because they are like scars on my brain. I would never wish that experience on anyone, and yet good things came from that time, too. It has made me the self-reflective person that I am today, and I will always recognize the patterns of dominate forces of persuasion. I can literally cringe with a feeling of alarm when I am near a person possessing an oppressive or controlling nature. Trusting people is a huge obstacle to overcome for anyone who has been victimized by a cult group. Those who have been preyed upon become sensitive to what is reality and what is fiction. We can spot the liars and their motives, and you can be sure that we will be the first ones to call them on it because we have known the evil behind their deceit.

I feel that "my best quality and my worst quality are the same. Blatant honesty!"

After being lied to and manipulated for a period of about six months, I was able to break free. It was not easy; it was like having withdrawals from drugs or alcohol. I was terrified, shaking and weeping. Coping with life would be difficult, and it took months to recover. To this day, the effects of what happened to me can bring up a feeling which causes a rebellious and defensive attitude to overtake me, and my response can catch unwitting people off guard. Many times, when I feel I have unjustly treated some unsuspecting person, I apologize, but rarely take the time to explain why my reaction was the way it was. Those who have been under that type of submissive mind control may also feel that way because it never quite leaves you.

Keep in your mind that if anyone or a group of people ever makes you denounce someone or something, run from that person or those persons and never look back. They are not your friends! Trusted allies are people who respect your ideas and enjoy a reasonable debate. They may try to convince you that their way is the best, but they should never condemn or shame you for expressing your feelings. Disagreement is normal, and to listen and understand each other's positions on issues is a healthy behavior. Mature confident thinkers are never too afraid to voice their opinion, and our First Amendment Right gives us that freedom.

The passion that I have for speaking up about the current issues plaguing our nation is due to the undeniable brainwashing that we are witnessing of our young adults. I recognize it! These millennials are leaving college campuses with the inability to function in the real world. Their Liberal professors have damaged these innocent ones beyond belief, and these instructors do not care one bit, it's their plan and they have an agenda. They want the Progressive Socialist ideology seared into our children's young brains. The college-educated young adults that we see come out of school today have some levels of cognitive brain damage, with symptoms ranging from mild liberal viewpoints to a full-on state, rendering them a mindless zombie. Please do not take this the wrong way, but if you leave a prestigious university and you find that you cannot cope with reality, chances are that you have been the victim of this wicked form of abuse. If you do not get your way and you find yourself needing a safe space, a blanket, and a cup of hot chocolate, chances are that you are a brainwashed zombie. And I should know because I have been there, too. "It ain't fun!"

*****

When I heard a presentation given by Dr. Lance Wallnau regarding his "Seven Mountains to Culture Transformation," it resonated with me as if a light had been turned on in a place of darkness. Wallnau's perspective comes from a biblical Christian point of view. I sometimes refer to Lance as the Tony Robbins for Christians; he is a best-selling author, educator, and coach. I highly recommend his books and teachings because he presents the messages so clearly and in an entertaining way. As he spoke, I immediately realized that the radical Left-Wing of the Democratic Party had been taking advantage of these areas of influence in our American culture to gain control of our government and our people.

Wealthy elitists and political geniuses, from around the world, have figured out that if they can take over the spheres of influence that affect the minds of their populous, then they can manipulate the ideology of their nations. Mind control verses free thinkers! Do you ever wonder why our youth cannot seem to cope with life? Do you ever wonder why there is so much confusion and depression? "Divide and conquer" is the mantra of those power-wielding rulers! They do not want you to think for yourself. Instead, they form your thoughts and then pander with pathetic groveling to gain your vote. Brainwashing tactics are a sadistic evil, being used to harm our societies. It is an incredibly cruel abuse of intimidation, used to advance an oppressive domination, destabilizing and destroying the well-being of the citizenry. They have become hell-bent on creating chaos throughout territories by promoting violence and fear. Their end game is their total control over our nations by demanding complete conformity from their victims to their one way of thinking and behaving. Thus, leaving us bound as their brainless slaves!

Though some might call my accusation a boldface conspiracy theory, woke groups of people have figured out that the Democratic Party has been taken over by power-mongering game players with activist mentalities. This hijacked Democrat Party is no longer your father and mother's party of John F. Kennedy. Soon after his assassination, these Left-Wing radicals started a movement to overtake and control America. Although each party has struggled for sole power since the original divide, which formed the two political parties, a quest for a one-party domination took full force in the late 1960s. The Democrat Party was the best target at that time for radicalization. However, my theory is not that the Democrats are the bad guys and the Republicans are the good guys, not at all. It was simply easier to control the Left over the Right. This also led to the ability to play each group against one another. Who are the "Bad Guys?" Those controllers of the nation's fate, the power-mongering political establishment elite, and the wealthy family dynasties and the business monopolies who fund them.

Activists, of the past sixty years, have gradually taken over most of the areas of influence that have formed the cultural habits of our modern-day American way of life. You can see these Radicals pushing a tangled web of control using their wild ideology throughout our educational systems, Hollywood, religious institutions, businesses, and so on. These changes throughout the past few decades have propelled us further and further to the extremely radicalized Liberal dogma. This continual push to the Far Left is driving us toward the Progressive's agenda of Communism and Socialism. The underlying objectives are ceasing total power and gaining oppressive domination to take control of the population and determine our futures, not only for America but for the entire world. It is crucial to these powerful elites to convince us that America is a bad place, which needs their ideological path for redemption. It is imperative to their mission that "We the People" no longer control this nation with our vote. You can see them trying to erase our history and abolish our laws, while slowly chipping away at more and more of our freedoms and our rights. Leading us down a path that will eventually destroy our beloved Constitution and our precious American Dream.

You and I are not at fault! We have gradually become their victims. They have played us like a fiddle and enslaved us as part of their designed plan. These thought manipulators will no longer control us or our children, if we take their power away. We can start by educating our children to be freethinkers, by sharing the knowledge of the persuasive tactics that may surround them. We can warn those we love of the possible deception in even trusted places because if the information they are receiving is not accurate, they can easily be manipulated in their way of thinking, taking away their ability to be a freethinker. Now that we have a keen sense of awareness, we can discern our true feelings and make smart decisions. But most importantly, we can be released from the stronghold of the oppressors who victimize us. Slaves no more!

For Thoughtful Consideration

1. Are we victims of our circumstances? Or are we stronger because of them?
2. Who have been the mentors in our lives? And how have they swayed your decisions?
3. Do you think that the extreme push in Hollywood for more perversion and violence have destroyed the innocence of our youth? Have those gradual extreme presentations of promiscuity, profanity, and bloodshed made it more acceptable in our culture?
4. Which areas of influence have been the most responsible for making you the person that you have become today?
5. Do you see the importance of being aware of those who can manipulate our children? And do you see the importance of teaching our youth to be wary of the messages those instructors promote?
6. Are we "free" thinkers? Does being aware of the forms of manipulation help us to be understanding of others?

CHAPTER 4

"We the People" of Common Sense

Never bite the hand that feeds you!

D o you ever listen to people who are known scholars or have wonderful credentials and think they do not seem very bright? How about the man or woman who has many college degrees with honors, but you cannot imagine them surviving for long on a deserted island? They call themselves intellectual elites.

Although they consider themselves much wiser than you, some of these people may make you wonder, "What on earth are they thinking?"

These geniuses are all around us, and even though they qualify as book smart, they may have little or no common sense. Americans had been intimidated by those type people and we trusted them because after all they told us, we were the dummies. These elites kept telling "We the People" that they were the intelligent ones, and if we stupid folks agreed with their ideology, we would appear to have made a brilliant choice. So when they told us that they could choose our rulers wisely, of course we would follow along like smart sheeple. Then, when their elite politicians made us loads of promises that they never planned to keep, we discovered that their political policies were not adequately designed to benefit the citizens of our nation. In the end, they appeared to be useless idiots. And suddenly, we did not care if they were even college educated, we just wished that they would try to use a little common sense when making decisions for us and our fellow Americans.

Common sense comes easy for some people. These people are usually simple thinkers. They do not overly complicate things. To say one has common sense may seem less impressive than to say one has honors and degrees of importance; however, lacking common sense is a form of stupidity regardless of one's stature in life. People are sometimes gifted with common sense. My husband has that gift, me not so much. I attribute that quality to my husband because he has a very keen sense of awareness and the ability to focus on one thing at a time, while I tend to be scattered with several tasks and driven to rush on to the next project. I truly admire Tom's ability to figure things out because he is observant in a way that most people may not be. Also, regarding our book-smart friends, sometimes we run the risk of overlooking what is right in front of us when our head is stuck in a book. You can follow a manual or you can learn by trial and error. Either way, the key is learning and retaining the lesson learned.

I have often said that if I had to be stranded with one person on a desert island, it would be my husband, Tom. Not just for the obvious reasons, but because he is so filled with common-sense smarts. Firstly, we would not starve because he can hunt it, kill it, clean it, and cook it. He would make sure that I do not inadvertently eat some poisonous berry or something. He could make sure we had a cozy shelter and build me a warm fire. He could keep us safe. I am sure he could engineer a way to get us home eventually. And miracle of miracles, my hero might even figure out a way to get me a cup of coffee each morning. Sounds like a nice fantasy, but my point is this: in life, you have people who excel at all kinds of different things; however, our brilliance is not limited to what grades we got in college or what title we hold, it comes from our individual talent and our ability to use it. Common sense is needed in every situation, but it does not take a genius in every situation!

We had watched the destruction of some of the most precious qualities of our nation in recent decades. They had slowly diminished before our eyes because we had let common sense escape our decision processes, which had led us to weak policies and selfish agendas. Let me give you a few simple analogies that I think could be useful in bettering the relations we have with each other, and the care we take from within our borders.

Let us use some common sense while considering the policies we need for running America to her greatest potential. Are the choices our leaders make that affect our ability as a nation to survive levelheaded? Can we say that the ruling class has our best interests in mind? Think of our country as if it were our personal family unit.

After a mother has a child, she may devote so much time to her child and husband that she forgets to take care of herself. We all know that if she gets too tired or even sick, that Mother is not much good for her family. In order to have a strong and well-adjusted family, the mother must take care of herself too. We want our mother to be happy and healthy. And in return, our mother loves us so deeply that she knows she must protect us and look out for our well-being. In the same way, America is no good to anyone if we do not take care of America by keeping her safe and strong. Taking it a bit further, we can still love our neighbor and want to help them when they need us because our love for our family does not take anything away from our feelings of generosity and compassion toward our neighbor.

Contemplate this: your child needs food and clothing, and you can barely make ends meet. You should not feel guilty because you chose to make sure your rent is paid, your child is fed and clothed, rather than give your neighbor your last loaf of bread. And one step further, building and saving for your children's futures is also an honorable thing to do. Never feel ashamed of your desire to better the quality of life for your family. Your neighbor may need to take care of themselves because you just do not have the means to help. Your ability to help your neighbor's situation may not have anything to do with your feelings toward your neighbor.

Another practical thought, if your neighbor is a violent child molester, you do not leave your door open at night. In fact, you might get a big vicious dog to protect your children. And moving or putting in a security system should not make you a racist, bigot, sexist, or phobic hater of any kind. Shaming people who choose to take care of their household first is not right, and the same can be said for the care we take of the citizens of our country. Keeping America safe and secure is simply common sense and a no-brainer!

Here is another no-brainer: if we are smart with our household expenses, even though we might have a modest budget that we must keep within, we know that exceeding our budget would be irresponsible and reckless. Ultimately, overspending could even prove dangerous to our ability to survive. On the other hand, being thrifty, saving money, and setting goals can lead to a prosperous future. In the same way, America needs to be mature in its ways of fiscal responsibility. Our current national debt has become out of control, and it is time for our politicians to make a change before it is too late. Common sense should tell you that you had better stop the wasteful spending. We do not have the money for Socialism. Period! Gifting is not in our budget.

Margaret Thatcher said it best when she said, "The problem with socialism is that you eventually run out of other people's money."

America will never be a Socialist nation. We are a people of great integrity and ingenuity. Ours is a country built on the American Dream, which means we are in a land of opportunities. We are a free people destined for endless possibilities. We can be proud because we do not take handouts. We are the people who care enough to give our neighbors a hand up when they need it. "We the People" living the motto of the American Way!

Our common-sense philosophy is if we can make America succeed, then we can help other countries succeed, but if we fail, we cannot help anyone. Our love for our nation does not take away from our love and respect for other nations. Quite the opposite, we can admire other nations, but can offer little if we are weak. Under this current pandemic crisis, all nations have become aware that it is crucial to be independent in a very self-sufficient way. We all must not rely on other countries for our well-being. And by being able to take care of one's own nation, we do not run the risk of needing to rely on other nations for our necessities.

In regard to another rational path of governing, I prefer the Conservative's approach to society's norms. While the Republican leaders give individuals the freedom they deserve, they expect the citizen to abide by the laws of the land. If the Liberal leaders give special consideration to those who are not just seeking freedom but also thinking that they should be free to break the law, that infringes on everyone else's ability to be free because it undermines basic fairness and puts people's safety at risk. Fairness for one group of people should never negatively hinder another group of people's abilities to succeed.

Another commonsense observation might be applied when treating citizens differently based on income equality. It is crucial to use our welfare system objectively and justly. Government programs supplying financial aid to an individual must make determinations of who can remain self-sufficient and who cannot maintain the ability to financially support themselves. A few considerations are a must, firstly the process of determining a true need and secondly the process of identifying the specific level of need.

There are also some cases of injustice that seem unreasonable to mindful citizens. One such injustice is that often a needy noncitizen gets rewarded some benefits funded by those who are law-abiding taxpayers. This can seem like a blatant slap in the face to the everyday hardworking American. An even worse scenario is when an illegal alien is let go for a crime that the citizen would be fully punished for, it is a gross miscarriage of justice. Sanctuary cities have become a contentious issue between the Right and the Left. My Conservative view is "Fairness for *all*! Your sanctuary cannot trump our safety!"

We have seen far too many angel families who have lost loved ones to illegal thugs. Common sense tells us that you do not cause your own family pain or put them in harm's way to help outsiders. Those who are looking to prove they are virtuous may want to do so at their own risk, but not at the risk of others. And most importantly, our desire for safety and security should never be misconstrued as a lack of compassion for those illegal immigrants who are good people, those who sincerely want to come to our country and abide by our laws.

These basic principle differences between Conservatives verses Liberals have not only caused the disunity of our people but fundamentally broken the forgotten middle class of the USA. Reasonable thinking tells us that we need to protect our middle class because they are the working men and women of America that give us the products and care that we depend on for our healthy lifestyles. Socialism destroys the middle class by creating a nation of the very wealthy and the very poor. While they promise the moon and the stars, they hold their constituents down, instead of helping them up. Their political agenda has proven to promote desperation and crime in the people who "have not" and gives the control of those people to the rich. These socialistic policies are designed so that the rich get richer and the poor get poorer, which means only the rich have any power and the ability to live the American Dream.

Welfare Justice

Most forgotten men and women would not begrudge those who are truly in need of any governmental assistance. We all must genuinely care for our citizens who have been less fortunate than us. Giving to those who have disabilities, preventing them from caring for themselves, or sharing with those who have befallen some crisis that has left them helpless is our American way. We must always put the needs of others as our primary duty, not only as an obligation, but as the compassionate nation that we are and always have been. And it is crucial that we never lose sight of the fact that we are a country based on strong ethics and values that lead us to maintain our ability to care for our people first so that we can be stronger for other nations as well.

As forgotten Americans, both Democrat and Republican, we had felt seriously let down by our government and the politicians who were our leaders. We had developed a deep lack of trust in our nation's institutions. We had watched our Republic's power slowly slip away from "We the People." And it had not gone unnoticed that there was a crushing disregard for the middle class and a flagrant unbalance in the fairness of the welfare state.

As a wife and mother of two, I worked from our home. This gave me the opportunity to make an income while taking care of my children, so we could have a little extra spending money. I remember in those days, my husband and I realized that daycare for our children would practically cost as much as any wage that I might earn, and we agreed that having one full-time parent would be a benefit for our family. In 2002, when my youngest girl was a toddler, a preschool was forming in our area. I contemplated sending her, so she could socialize with other children and learn to take direction from a teacher. I was told my child's fee would be $18 a day, coming to $360 a month. At that time, it would be within our budget for us to send our daughter, although it would mean pinching our pennies. We were very tempted, but ultimately, we decided to pass. One of the deciding factors was that the tuition was based on income, and lower income families were receiving free tuition. When we found out that a few of our friends were getting free tuition for their children and consequently sending more than one child, I must admit that it did bother me a bit. Two of the family's fathers were working for wages that would be described as under the table, which was tax-free money and did not show up as an income, so they could claim to be low-income families. Now, I do realize it is up to the individual to be honest when claiming their income. I even understand why these families could justify taking advantage of the system because the tuition would be a hardship for any middle-class family such as ourselves. However, would it not have been lovely if we all just paid $9 a day for our children, and each child's monthly tuition would have been half at $180? How come those who were cheating the system were the ones being rewarded? My sense of fairness said, "I do not need a handout, but it would be nice to get a break in the cost!"

Forgotten men and women realize that sometimes life just is not all that fair and balanced. Later, when my daughters were in middle school, they both needed braces on their teeth. I told my husband that I would have the opportunity to take on a second job as a bookkeeper, while still managing to be a full-time mom. I was excited to be able to use the extra income to pay for my oldest daughter to get through the first two years of dental work and then work for my youngest daughter's following two years. By taking the secretary bookkeeper position, it was a blessing to not have to struggle financially, but I sure was tired and grumpy a great deal of the time. I remember being relieved to get to a place where I could start thinking of passing the extra job off to someone who might love the income. I had a neighbor who complained of needing extra money, and she seemed quite bored. Of course, I thought of her immediately for the secretary bookkeeper work. I told her, "This job is nice and easy. It takes about ten hours a week and you can work out your own schedule, anytime of day. Plus, I would be happy to fully train you."

Her reply was "No, it would mess up my disability."

I found out that she also made more money on welfare. I realized that the government only gave her enough income to barely get by, but if she made a few extra dollars on her own, the government would just deduct those dollars from her disability aid. The absolute saddest part of this story is that unknown to me, her boredom and severe depression had been driving her to drink massive amounts of hard alcohol. Several months later, she was found near death.

It became clear to me that the welfare system has not been designed to give folks the incentive to earn more money, which could eventually lift them out of poverty. Here is my observation, those in the middle class are paying full price and taxed more with no reward for their hard work and self-sufficiency, while the poor are awarded an income that keeps them impoverished. So forgotten men and women are being beaten down, while the poverty stricken are being held down. This income inequality must stop! However, not by the means of Socialism, which would cripple our society even more. Changes should be implemented with an overhaul of our government's welfare system, using balanced and fair judgment.

*****

For a couple reasons, I always hoped that my girls would go to college. I really enjoyed my years being a college student. As a young adult, I think it is important to have time to explore your destiny and what better way than to get off on your own. Also, it is undeniable that a proper education is valuable, no matter what path you choose in life. Both of my daughters had a different plan though. My oldest, Lacey, started working in one of our family member's businesses, and she was able to learn a lot on the job. With that experience behind her, she was offered to work for Pacific, Gas & Electric, the energy company in California. Regardless of PG&E's problems, they give wonderful benefits and nice wages to their employees. Learning a trade and finding a quality company to work for be a blessing to any family. My youngest, Rachel, started out at a junior college near home, to see what she might find interesting to do with her future. However, college did not seem like the choice for her either. She has been working as a teacher's aide at a local grammar school and thinking about teaching as a career option. And Rachel knows that attending a university can still be a viable choice for her, we would still be happy to help her with the expense.

College tuition is another touchy subject for me because I think costs should be less for all students. In my opinion, it is not logical in the way the administrators determine the amounts of tuition and qualifications for granting scholarships or financial aid. The expense of a college education has become enormous, and like the government, these institutions cater to the very wealthy and the very poor, leaving the forgotten Americans behind. Middle-class families are not capable of paying those kinds of tuitions without taking on a burden of lifelong saving or the major hardship of debt. Students who pay their own way through school are left with hefty student loans and debts that sometimes handicap them for years. And as "We the People" struggle, we witness the injustice of an illegal immigrant being awarded a full scholarship or a celebrity cheats the system to get their child a free ride at a prestigious university. Yep, while the taxpayer gets no relief, they fund those who are not citizens or those who are cheating the system. It is an outrage! Do not let this bother you though, because you would not want to appear uncompassionate. And let us not forget, it all comes back to the socialist mentality which lacks all common sense, they bankrupt the forgotten men and women while unfairly rewarding those who are unworthy.

Moving forward, common sense tells us that incentivizing our millennials to succeed is crucial. They need to see a reason to change the trends of entitlement and victimization. We need them to learn the importance of having basic principles of fairness and honor by making a strong work ethic and desire to save toward their futures something to be rewarded. Teaching them the conservative value of giving a bonus for a job well done rather than a prize to those who have not earned it. Offering to support them with opportunities for prosperity, not entitling them to an alternate reality of gifts without merit. We need to instruct them how not to become slaves to their circumstances, but to pick themselves up, to be strong and resilient. Showing them that pride comes with finding the ability to cope in situations that sometimes are not of our liking. Bringing them up to be responsible and respectful young adults is one of the most loving and compassionate things that we can do for our children and grandchildren.

For Thoughtful Consideration

Does there seem to be a lack of common sense by our government's bureaucrats in dealing with our country's issues? We all have different ideas about policies that can benefit our citizenry. Which of those policies do you see working smoothly, if any?

Some of the scenarios I have used in this chapter, and others like them, do apply to many of the problems that plague our government's welfare system. Most of these welfare systems and funded programs have become so unfairly balanced. I would like to see some common sense–type solutions and changes that would benefit everyday forgotten citizens, as well as the poor and the needy proportionately. Do you see ways that we can care for all of people without hurting some in the process?

My sense of fairness and the difference between what was right and wrong starts to overtake me and the lady justice warrior in me thinks, "There has got to be a fairer way to share the benefits that our communities have to offer. We should not handicap one family or reward another based on anything other than need. And if someone struggles by needing two or three jobs to survive while someone else gets a free ride, that is not income equality, it is simply one-sided."

Lastly, cleaning up deception is crucial. You can use all the common sense in the world; however, if that world is filled with dishonesty, we all lose! Please do not be afraid to call the liars out! Truth and justice are the American Way!

CHAPTER 5

Political Victims

*True peace is not merely the absence of
tension; it is the presence of justice.*
—Martin Luther King Jr. in 1958

"We the People" have heard charming words of manipulation and lies from corrupt politicians, who have only one intention, and that is to gain our beloved *vote*! It is *all* about our *vote*! Yes, it is that simple! We are being *used*! Most politicians are *not* our friends!

In the current political environment, we are being targeted daily. There are powers of persuasion all around us, some intentional and other unintentional. Once we wake up to the tug-of-war political games, that we have been thrust in the middle of since the time we could cast our vote, we will understand that we have simply been victims of a majority of politicians that claim to care about us. Instead, they have enslaved us with their poor policies which are designed to keep us under their control. Ultimately securing our future *vote*!

Now, I am not going to say that there are *no* good politicians. In fact, I think that there are probably some fine politicians, hero types who would like to make a positive difference in the lives of their constituents. Some may even truly care about the impoverished who rely on their government for basic needs. And I am sure that several leaders would like to leave a better place in which their children and grandchildren can live. However, many politicians have played dirty, and now they have crossed the line. When these politicians become candidates, most of them become mudslinging barbarians, and "We the People" get caught up in the proverbial mud. Sometimes, we start slinging the mud with our preferred candidate. And, my friends, that is why we have friends and family members who choose to never to talk about politics. When in all actuality, we should be discussing the critical choices that hinder our safety and benefit ourselves and our communities. Our voices and our votes are crucial to the preservation of our republic!

The Radical Leftists

"Divide and conquer" technique has been a tactic used by powerful rulers and governments throughout the ages. The one implementing this strategy breaks up groups of people who threaten their power, by causing divisions. The use of this "divide and conquer" method is meant to control and dominate others so that the leader and/or ruling class can gain and maintain its power. One element of this concept involves fostering distrust and animosity been people to prevent their alliances with one another and invoke their loyalty to the provocateur. These tactics are ruthless and calculating, and America and her citizens have been targeted viciously not only by foreign actors, but also from within. Identifying who those actors are and ending their oppressive reign will be the first step in healing our nation.

In a prior chapter, I mentioned that most of the problems we are having with divisions among Americans has not been the result of one political party or the other. Most Liberals and Conservatives are people of integrity and morals. However, it is the fringe element of each group that have provoked strife and anger within their ideologies. The fringe element of the Liberals and Conservatives have been manipulated and played by the very corrupt entities who intentionally "divide and conquer." These cabals of powerful elites have seen the best way to achieve their goals through the choice to infiltrate one group and radicalize that group. These deceivers specifically preyed upon the Democratic Party. It was the easiest target because it aligned most closely with their agenda. By radicalizing the Far Left Wing, the wealthy cabal could get these political radicals to do their wicked bidding. Understanding the deception, recognizing the games, and knowing that we have become their victims is the first step in our forgiving each other, working together, and taking back our country. This awareness gives us power and strength. We become woke! And we offer this wokeness when we share this awareness by what has become known as nudging people we care about to take the red pill!

As we discussed previously, there are main areas of influence that have molded America's culture. These masterful guiders of our civilization come from our churches, businesses, government, academia, media, arts, and entertainment. Radical Liberals have been manipulating the minds of our American people by taking over our schools, the mainstream media, and Hollywood to influence our culture. If someone is told by their family members, their peer group, their political leaders, and/or their favorite celebrities that they should think a certain way politically, then they run the risk of becoming swayed to a certain political ideology. If this ideology is based on lies and deceptions, they run the risk of feeling, acting, and thinking passionately about false narratives. These unaware people have become political victims because they have trusted and admired dishonest people. Currently, we are surrounded by political victims. Most of these political victims have no idea that they have been misled. Some believe the lies that they have been fed over and over again. In some cases, these gross deceptions can incite fear and anger, sometimes leading to violence and destruction. And the outcome is never a good one.

Saul Alinsky was an American community and political activist who wrote the book *Rules for Radicals* in 1971. This playbook has been the Democrat Party's guide, and we have been their victims. Below are some familiar highlights of Alinsky's twelve rules, which we have seen the Radical Liberals using throughout the few decades.

1. "Power is not only what you have, but what the enemy thinks you have." Power is derived from two main sources—money and people. "Have-nots" must build power from flesh and blood.
2. "Never go outside the expertise of your people." It results in confusion, fear, and retreat. Feeling secure adds to the backbone of anyone.
3. "Whenever possible, go outside the expertise of the enemy." Look for ways to increase insecurity, anxiety, and uncertainty.
4. "Make the enemy live up to its own book of rules." Example: If the rule is that every letter must get a reply, send thirty thousand letters. You can kill them with this because no one can possibly obey all their own rules.
5. "Ridicule is a man's most potent weapon." There is no defense. It's irrational. It's infuriating. It also works as a key pressure point to force the enemy into confessions.
6. "A good tactic is one your people enjoy." They'll keep doing it and will even suggest better ones.
7. "A tactic that drags on too long becomes a drag." Don't become old news.
8. "Keep the pressure on. Never give up." Keep trying new things to keep the opposition off balance. As the opposition masters one approach, hit them from the flank with something new.
9. "The threat is usually more terrifying than the thing itself." Imagination and ego can dream up many more consequences than any activist.
10. "The major premise for tactics is the development of operations that will maintain a contact pressure upon the opposition." It is this unceasing pressure that results in the reactions from the opposition that are essential for the success of the campaign.
11. "If you put a negative hard enough, it will push through and become a positive." Violence from the other side can

win the public to your side because the public sympathizes with the underdog.

12. "The price of a successful attack is a constructive alternative." Never let the enemy score points because you're caught without a solution to the problem.

13. "Pick the target, freeze it, personalize it, and polarize it." Cut off the support network and isolate the target from sympathy. Go after people, not institutions; people hurt faster than institutions.

Wow! Saul sounds like a horrible monster! There must be no doubt that a follower of his would be equally as horrible. And yet you see the similarities of the tactics of the Radical Left Wing of the Democrat Party. They have employed some of these strategies for decades, and recently, they have intensified to become a maximum pressure campaign.

Saul Alinsky also was an advocate of Socialism. Does any part of his views below sound appealing to you? Keep in mind, he said, "The first is the most important."

1. Healthcare—Control the people's health and you control the people.

2. Poverty—Increase the poverty level as high as possible; poor people are easier to control and will not fight back if you give them what they need to live.

3. Debt—Increase the debt to an unsustainable level. That way, you can increase taxes, which in turn will generate even more poverty.

4. Gun Control—Remove the ability of people to defend themselves from the government. That way you can create a police state.

5. Welfare—Take control of every aspect of a person's life (food, housing, jobs and income).

6. Education—Take control of what people read and listen to; take control of what children study in school.

7. Religion—Remove the belief in God from government and schools.

8. Class Warfare—Divide the people into wealthy and poor. This will cause discontent and make it easier to increase taxes across the board without losing the support of the poor by making everyone think you will only tax the rich!

In America, many of the above targets have been achieved successfully. In Italy and other member states of the European Union, all the targets have been achieved for quite some time now, except for the United Kingdom, which has recently opted out of the European Union. The overwhelming theme of Saul Alinsky's mission was one of total control and domination. Do you see how it lines up with the direction that the Far-Left Wing of the Democratic Party have been heading?

*****

The Democrat Party is no longer the party of JFK. I have so many of my moderate Democrat friends tell me how they have not left their party, but their party has left them. And that is what has inspired groups such as the Walk Away Movement, which was started by Brandon Straka. #WalkAway is a social media group that has encouraged other woke Democrats to leave their party. This Walk Away campaign has hundreds of testimonies from likeminded individuals, who have become disillusioned with the misdirection of the Democrat Party and their Far-Left Liberal ideology.

Recognizing tactics of radical opponents gives you an edge that they were not expecting. It is crucial that we and our fellow citizens are aware of these forms of manipulation, so we can make sure that they do not overpower us, with their intention of taking our government away from "We the People."

In 1958, Cleon Skousen wrote *The Naked Communist* in which he had forty-five goals to overthrow the United States. Some of these goals are strategies that we can see the Radial Left are employing today. See if you can spot some of the ways in which communism has already infiltrated our free country and how it is currently manipulating our society. A few highlights include:

1. Capture one of the political parties in the US.
2. Weaken basic American institutions by claiming their activities violate civil rights.
3. Get controls of the school. Use them as transmission belts for Socialism and current Communist propaganda. Soften the curriculum. Get control of the Teachers' Associations. Put the party line in textbooks.
4. Gain control of all student newspapers
5. Use student riots to foment public protests against programs or organizations which are under Communist attack.
6. Infiltrate the press.
7. Gain control of key positions in radio, TV, and motion pictures.
8. Continue discrediting American culture by degrading all forms of artistic expression. An American Communist was told to "eliminate all good sculpture from parks and buildings, substitute shapeless, awkward and meaningless forms."
9. Control art critics and directors of art museums. "Our plan is to promote ugliness, repulsive, meaningless art."
10. Eliminate all laws governing obscenity by calling them censorship and a violation of free speech and free press.
11. Break down cultural standards of morality by promoting pornography and obscenity in books, magazines, motion pictures, radio, and TV.
12. Present homosexuality, degeneracy, and promiscuity as "normal, natural, healthy."
13. Infiltrate the churches and replace revealed religion with "social" religion. Discredit the Bible, and emphasize the need for intellectual maturity, which does not need a "religious crutch."
14. Eliminate prayer or any phase of religious expression in the schools on the ground that it violates the principle of "separation of church and state."

15. Discredit the American Constitution by calling it inadequate, old-fashioned, out of step with modern needs, a hindrance to cooperation between nations on a worldwide basis.
16. Discredit the Founding Fathers. Present them as selfish aristocrats who had no concern for the "common man."
17. Belittle all forms of American culture and discourage the teaching of American history on the ground that it was only a minor part of the "big picture."
18. Support any Socialist movement to give centralized control over any part of the culture—education, social agencies, welfare programs, mental health clinics, etc.
19. Infiltrate and gain control of more trade unions.
20. Discredit the family as an institution. Encourage promiscuity and easy divorce.
21. Emphasize the need to raise children away from the negative influence of parents. Attribute prejudices, mental blocks, and retarding of children to suppressive influence of parents.

These authoritarian principles not only take away the liberties of a free people, but they crush any spirit of the dreams we hold dear and a pursuit of happiness that is the American Way. This viewpoint of Communism leads to the complete destruction of the foundations of Western cultures. The Radical Left has been cheapening our American values and beliefs for the last few decades, and you can see that growing more evident and extreme with time.

Progressivism is an elite view that "We the People" are incapable of making our own decisions. Those elite dislike, disrespect, and they have contempt for everyday Americans. While they pretend to care and have compassion for the citizen, they control and manipulate the people by imposing burdensome taxes, strict regulations, and oppressive laws. This handicaps the public to the point where they are no longer free. Under the overbearing rules of the Progressive Elite's agenda the government makes all the decisions for its citizens.

Socialism, Communism, and Progressivism are all the political, social, and economic philosophies that have become the movement of the Liberal Left, which has taken over whatever was left of any moderate Democrat Party. Their positive twist on these philosophies is that their government will compassionately take care of its people, and if you oppose their view, you are not compassionate. Most of these types of governments have only two extremes: very poor people and very rich people. Their middle classes are destroyed and cease to exist. Liberal cities across our nation have proven to be great examples of the way democrat policies have become, leaving their residents with heartbreak, homeless populations, severe poverty, filthy unsanitary conditions, rundown infrastructures, and unsafe environmental issues. And then living amongst all that, you have the wealthiest elites, who are the powerful ruling class.

That is not America! That is not who we are as a people, Americans!

Nationalism vs. Globalism

You would not think that having pride in our country could be twisted into being a bad or selfish thing, and yet it has been by our radicalized Democrat brothers and sisters. They call us racist and xenophobic. However, we know that loving and caring for our nation does not mean that we do not have respect for other nations. It was Cesar Chavez who said, "Preservation of one's own culture does not require contempt or disrespect for other cultures."

This nationalism was a major disruptor to the status quo of globalism, which had been taking over the world. As patriots, we have joined forces to take back the American government and her bureaucracies to place it firmly in the hands of its people. Since this patriotic movement has taken place, the Radical Left has fought back with a vicious resistance, playing into the hands of the greedy power-monger politicians.

Populism is another term that fits into the America First Agenda. Its ideology is based on the people having control over the ruling class, who are there to serve the people. Populism can easily be combined and closely knit with this current Nationalist Movement. Both are completely at odds with globalism, which promotes the whole world merging political and economic alliances. Let us just say that, a Populist and Nationalist's policies entirely shut down the Globalist agenda. So you can see why it is crucial for the Globalists to resist and destroy the Nationalist at all costs, and they do this by dividing the citizenry and causing strife between them. These political resisters use victims and create victims.

*****

We have been political victims for so long that some of us do not even realize it. Politicians do a few things to use victims. As an example, the politician charms the victim and tells them that they will make their lives better. Then that same politician tells this victim that their opponent is a despicable human being that hates them and will make their lives miserable. And then, to divide the people, the politician tells the victim that not only is their opponent awful, but so are their opponent's supporters. Before you know it, everyone has sided up against each other thinking the very worse and hateful things about each other. Are you following me? Does it sound familiar?

Politicians also create victims. It is true! Think about it. Did you ever think that there could be so many phobias? My friends, most people love each other and their neighbor. I mean this! You know that there are bad people, but come on, I think it is rare. Politicians *need* you to be a victim, so they can *use* you to make themselves look virtuous and morally superior. If you support them and *vote* for them, they tell you that you too can be virtuous and morally superior. However, if you support their opponent, they will label you a racist, bigot, xenophobic, homophobic, sexist, fascist, and every other hater that you can think exists. It is called identity politics, and it is ruining us.

You have heard it, over and over, this politician is playing the race card or the gender card. Religious groups are being targeted for their beliefs. Your ideas and my ideas may differ however the well-being of our country should always remain the same. Identity politics is not only dividing us, it is based on standards that are not American. Those of us who are true Americans know that we are a melting pot of diversity, which includes different ideals within our nation. It is our constitutional rights to have different thoughts and our freedoms to be unique that unite us as one American people. This is what make us an exceptional country!

Please Consider This

Will we ever stop believing the vicious lies of political adversaries that are meant to divide us? None of us should be labeled by race, gender, or creed. We should unite simply as Americans. When will we finally live up to the standard of the great Martin Luther King Jr.'s words, "I have a dream that my four children will one day live in a nation where they will not be judged by the color of their skin, but the content of their character?"

The key take away for "We the People" who have become political victims is that, we can let the politicians duke it out with each other and let them bring each other down; however, we must reject their lies and deceit by not letting them destroy us and our unity as people and as a nation. Remember, those politicians work for us and should be held accountable to us. We are Americans who battle every day to make a better life for our families, our communities, and our country, and we are all in this together. Let us not let anyone tell us otherwise!

CHAPTER 6

My Trump Story

As long as you're going to be thinking anyway, think big.
—Donald Trump

A fter the very contentious presidential election of 2016, I thought that, I could just breathe a long sigh of relief, celebrate, and get a well-deserved break. However, there was a lingering voice inside me that said it was not going to be that simple. And almost immediately, I was aware that although the election had been won, there was a resistance that was brewing.

First, I would like to share with you what got me to Election Day on November 8, 2016. I had never been a Donald Trump fan. Our family had never watched the hit TV show *The Apprentice*. In fact, I may have had a poor opinion of Donald Trump based on his "You're Fired!" boorish persona. I knew he was an extremely rich and successful businessman and that he was quite the playboy womanizer, but that was all.

In the summer of 2015, I started thinking about who I would be supporting for the upcoming presidential race. I had been involved in politics and conservative movements for the previous ten years. In 2012, I focused much of my efforts on helping Mitt Romney and Paul Ryan by doing my share of what I called unofficial campaigning. This time around, I realized conservatives were going to need to step up their efforts, then find a candidate who would be strong and charismatic. We conservatives had some good choices. Particularly appealing to me were Dr. Ben Carson, Senator Ted Cruz, Senator Marco Rubio, Governor Mike Huckabee, and Governor Rick Perry (not necessarily in that order).

It was August 6, 2015, the night of the first Republican Primary Debate. My husband, Tom, and I sat down with much anticipation, hoping that we would both agree upon our favorite candidate. I'll never forget the moment that Donald Trump took the stage, I said something like, "Donald Trump! What is Donald Trump doing? He is not even a politician. Is he?"

Tom's response was similar in a "Is this a joke?" manner.

As we watched the debate, we laughed and enjoyed the banter from Donald Trump and his opponents.

Surprisingly, we began to agree with the things coming from Donald Trump's mouth. As the first debate concluded, I said to my husband, "Who did you like the best?"

And he replied decisively, "Donald Trump!"

In amazement, I said, "I know, I did too! What was that?"

We agreed that Donald Trump sounded strong, firm, and on target regarding making America better for the hardworking Americans like us, who have felt pushed aside for many years. It was refreshing to know that someone else sympathized with everyday citizens, who were feeling powerless. "We the People" who knew that our government was no longer "of and for the people," knew that we would never achieve what was once called the American Dream, if we let the current political establishment rule our land.

*****

Apparently, I had missed it, but over two decades ago, Oprah Winfrey interviewed Donald Trump. He spoke of his disappointment with the way our nation had been being run by politicians. She asked him if he would ever run for president. Trump said, "If it got so bad, I would never want to rule it out totally because I really am tired of seeing what's happening with this country."

This successful businessman found that day had come! A day in which, we were getting away from the principles of our US Constitution and its Bill of Rights. A day in which we were losing sight of our middle class and our hardest working men and women. A day in which lawlessness seemed acceptable and being virtuous was being condemned. A day in which America needed a businessman, not another shady politician. A day in which "We the People" needed a miracle, and God provided a hero!

*****

The Progressive Socialists and the Liberal media were out to destroy Trump with a "no mercy" approach. Never taking him as a serious candidate. They mocked and belittled him, said he would never be our president. In February 2016, even Obama said of Trump, "I continue to believe that Mr. Trump will not be president."

I began to listen to Donald Trump and the other candidates whenever I got the opportunity; it became addicting for me. Sometimes, he would say something colorful and bold that was immediately up for debate and exaggerated beyond belief. It became apparent that he was going to be the punching bag with constant jabbing, ridicule, and lies. The more his attackers punched, he counterpunched with a stronger punch, leaving some of his tormenters knocked out. I felt myself defending him as if he were the ever appealing underdog.

*****

I loved this example from an unknown author because it truly summed up how many frustrated voters had been feeling in the fall of 2016. Here is the story; imagine this:

> You've been on vacation for two weeks, you come home, and your basement is infested with raccoons. Hundreds of rabid, messy, mean raccoons have overtaken your basement. You want them gone immediately. You call the city and 4

different exterminators, but nobody could handle the job. But there is this one guy and he guarantees you that he will get rid of the raccoons, so you hire him. You don't care if the guy smells, you don't care if the guy swears, you don't care if he's an alcoholic, you don't care how many times he's been married, you don't care if he voted for Obama, you don't care if he has plumber's crack...you simply want those raccoons gone! You want your problem fixed! He is the guy! He's the best—period!

Here's why we want Trump, yes he's a bit of an ass, yes he's an egomaniac, but we don't care. The county is a mess because of politicians, the Republican and Democratic Parties are two-faced and gutless, and illegals are everywhere.

We want it all fixed! We don't care that Trump is crude, we don't care that he insults people, we don't care that he had been friendly with Hillary, we don't care that he has changed positions, we don't care that he's been married three times, we don't care that he fights with Megan Kelly and Rosie O'Donnell, we don't care that he doesn't know the name of some Muslim Terrorist, etc. This county is weak, bankrupt, our enemies are making fun of us, we are being invaded by illegals, we are becoming a nation of victims where every Tom, Ricardo and Hassid is a special group with special rights to a point, where we don't even recognize the country we are born and raised in; "AND WE JUST WANT IT FIXED" and Trump is the only guy who seems to understand what the people want. We are sick of politicians, sick of the Democratic Party, Republican Party and sick of illegals. We just want this thing fixed. Trump may not be a saint, but he doesn't have lobbyist money holding him, he doesn't have political correctness restraining him, all you know is that he has been very successful, even though he has had failures. He is a good negotiator, he has built a lot of things, he's not a politician and he's definitely not a cowardly politician. And he says he'll fix it. And we believe him because he is too much of an egotist to be proven wrong.

Also we don't care if the guy has bad hair.

We just want those stinking raccoons gone—out of our house!

AND WE WANT THEM OUT NOW!

Although I did not write that analogy, it resonated with much of the way I had been feeling at that time. He was not that crude exterminator, but even if he had been, we would not have cared. We were not concerned how he would do it, we just wanted him to get the job done. Every day, forgotten men and women knew that we needed someone who would fight for us. We saw President Trump as more of a superhero who would battle the corrupt underworld on behalf of "We the People."

*****

President Obama did not care about us, he ignored us! He was popular with his base, and he was only a president for his Liberal people, not the average American people. We hoped that Obama would have kept his promises to clean up the inner cities with his Liberal policies. We hoped that he would have ended the oppressive traps which were creating more crime and more poverty in the African American communities. He certainly had the chance. We gave him eight years. But no, Obama just retreated and blamed Bush as he kept failing. Instead, Obama was more of an activist leader for those who had become indoctrinated in a hate for America, and he was their superhero.

I never understood why President Obama did not cease the opportunity to become the greatest president of our generation, he certainly had the potential. However, his popularity was more fitting of that of a celebrity. Being the cool, charismatic, and charming man that he was, he managed to win the hearts of millennials and Progressives across the country. He was the one president who could have put a stop to the evil of racism forever. I thought that because he was a black and white president, he could unite our citizenry, once and for all. But no, Obama was not the president for all. He always took sides in almost everything. He was not inclusive, he was divisive. Yes! Obama could have been a hero, a man worthy of being the Martin Luther King Jr. of our day. Sadly, he chose to be cocky, arrogant, and politically motived. And he chose the power of globalism over the well-being of the country that he was supposed to be leading.

$$*****$$

So we had a choice between Hillary Clinton, who would continue the downward spiral of the Obama administration, or Donald Trump, who was a successful businessman with the promise of something better. "We the People" chose the disrupter, who may have been a wild card, but we were willing to take the chance. He seemed real, refreshing, bold, and fearless. He was not ignoring the forgotten man and women, and we liked being the center of attention for a change. What did we have to lose? We would give him our vote!

As the campaigning progressed, we would hear and read beautiful stories of the many people Donald Trump had helped, and the major successes that he had accomplished over the years, but those stories were being hidden by his haters. While the media and his opponents portrayed him in more egregious ways with each passing day, his supporters could see that he was the opposite. Trump was a smart businessman with great ideas for our decaying nation, and he truly cared about the state of our country and the well-being of her people. But the constant attacks on Trump started to make us angry, which inadvertently caused us to become more disgusted with his attackers than we were with him. We defended him more fervently, and we began to love him all that much more. And that is how most of the Trump supporters became so loyal to him and each other. We began to bond and care for one another because we could see and feel the injustice of the lies and deception being forcefully thrown at Trump and us every day. His presidential campaign became a patriotic movement, and Trump became the strong leader that we needed for such a time as this!

In April 2016, my unofficial campaigning began. Like many other Trump supporters, we knew getting the truth out was crucial to contradict the false narratives. Our patriotic movement was growing, and we were gaining courage in the numbers. We were a peace-loving group that simply wanted the best for our country and *all* Americans. We knew that, there was nothing wrong with wanting a stronger economy and national security. We hoped that we finally would have an opportunity to return the power of our government to its people, and you could see the public's eyes begin to open with an awareness that we might actually get our country back. Suddenly, you could see that our challenge was no longer Democrat versus Republican, but it had become the Deep State Washington DC Swamp versus "We the People." It became an appealing goal! The more the corrupt establishment politicians, liberal mainstream media, and Hollywood opposers lambasted us and called us stupid, we proved them wrong. They showed us fake polls, while we were witnessing massive crowds at the Trump rallies. We knew that they were either the stupid ones or blatant liars, and either way, we knew that they were the bad guys. Those intimidating morons told us that we would never win, yet we are "winning, winning, winning!" We not only won the 2016 election, we proceeded to make the snobby naysayers cry, and we rocked the entire freakin' world!

Stick with me because shortly, I will be sharing with you the ways in which we can benefit America by unofficially and officially campaigning for patriotic political candidates. Choosing them based on their honesty and integrity, not their political party. Determining those men or women who will best represent their constituency in the "America First" way that our Founding Fathers intended. "We the People" have an important role in "Making America Great Again and Keeping America Great!"

CHAPTER 7

Fake News

Freedom of Speech is always under attack by Fascist mentality.
—Lawrence Ferlinghetti

S uddenly, you become aware of their tricks and deceit. I can remember the two events that gradually made my blinders start to come off because they bothered me so much. Yes, my friends, it was in two very heated "How dare they?" moments that I got my passion for politics. I might have been more forgiving if it had only happened once. We have heard it so many times, but I'll say it again, "Fool me once, shame on you. Fool me twice, shame on me." So now, you will fool me no more!

The first wake-up call, I do not remember the exact moment; however, I began sensing that something was not quite right. It was when Governor Sarah Palin was chosen as a running mate for 2008 presidential candidate Senator John McCain. You could see the mainstream media and Hollywood go after her in an unprecedented way that made observers aware that they were in collusion with the Democrat Party. Sarah was someone I greatly admired, and I thought she was brilliant at articulating what Conservative voters wanted. She made Senator Joe Biden look slow and unpolished, as he fumbled to find his words from notes. And then, as if the Left knew she was an existential threat, I watched the mainstream media and Hollywood destroy her character without any mercy. The way they viciously treated Sarah Palin was a preview of how maliciously they have been treating Donald Trump. These two compelling heroes of the Right needed to be destroyed by the Left or they would run the risk of losing not only their power but their corrupt ways. However, when Donald Trump emerged, he did not go down as planned and that made the Left go crazy. And to this day, the more President Trump fights back and wins, the crazier and more vicious the Left gets.

The second eye-opener, I remember the night so vividly. My husband was downstairs watching the local TV news, and I was listening from upstairs, while getting ready for bed. Our bedroom is a loft-style room, so I could hear perfectly as one of the commentators spoke about Christian haters in such as grotesque way while spewing twisted versions of the truth. It was at that moment God put the desire for me to follow politics more closely, in my heart. I do not know about you, but for me, when I see an injustice or lie being spread about someone else, I cannot let it go until I see justice being done. You could hear me roar, "That is such bull$#i+! Christians are lovers, not haters!"

I could be heard defending Christianity, as the religion that teaches its flock to give generously to others and to love unconditionally. I have spent the last decade vocalizing the proof of my statements. Simultaneously, I became the defender of the wrongly accused. An impassioned feisty woman arose. My shocked children asked me, "When did you get so interested in politics, Mom?"

And they have also said, "We don't remember you even liking politics."

I told them, "When I started to realize that we run the risk of losing our country if we do not get involved and try to save it. I knew I must get aware of what is going on and find ways to make a difference. I want you girls and my grandchildren to enjoy the freedoms and opportunities that this country has given me and has promised to offer you."

Journalism is not true reporting of the facts, like it used to be. Maybe it never was? Dishonest Liberal propagandists have infiltrated the mainstream media. They are *not* objective journalists. They are *not* noble truth seekers. And they are *not* people of high moral standards or integrity who give us simply the facts. Donald Trump did not make these bumbling reporters unworthy, he just exposed them for the appalling fakers that they have been for a long time.

I am not sure when the first time President Trump used the term "fake news"; however, it nailed the way most of his supporters had been feeling about the mainstream media for years. Do you feel that he is justified in using the term "fake news"? Let us examine President Trump's case against these TV networks and their reporters. The CNN and MSNBC networks give 95 percent negative coverage of President Trump daily. They do not cover positive stories or list his accomplishments, very often, if at all. Their so-called journalists speak to the president in rude and condescending tones, and they endlessly ask him "gotcha" style questions. Their disrespectful commentators have lied and labeled Trump and his supporters in very vicious ways, not only to sway audiences, but in some cases to provoke hatred and anger in their viewers. These news organizations often share the same talking points each day, and you can hear their mockingbird style verbiage recycled throughout their airwaves. Twisting Trump's words, taking them out of context, and cherry-picking to create a false narrative. Putting likeminded people around themselves, who will collaborate their deception, helps to convince you that you heard what you heard, thus forming your negative opinion. It bears repeating: true journalism has been dead for years. Even those that label themselves as journalists and try to stick to the facts show their biases in their demeanor and facial expressions. The way some of the Liberal media have treated President Trump is shameful. No journalist could have ever been as disrespectful to President Obama and gotten away with it. These nasty self-important reporters and commentators seem to think that it is okay, but it is not.

On July 3, 2020, when President Trump and First Lady Melania Trump visited Mount Rushmore, they were a stunning couple. Our gorgeous and classy First Lady wore a beautiful dress. I remember admiring the exquisite pattern of black twirling print with a white background. However, almost immediately, Melania Trump was mocked throughout social media by vicious trolls who said the dress looked as if President Trump scribbled with a Sharpie all over his wife's dress. In all actuality, the designer, Alexander McQueen, fashioned the dress for his Spring 2020 Collection and enlisted the help of English design students from Central Saint Martins in London, during a life-drawing class to make illustrations. The obnoxious classless agitators in the media and their endless cruelty have been an eye opener for the general public. We can see the truth about who are the belligerent and intolerant group, and it is the Left-Wing mean-spirited sore losers. We have an eloquent lovely woman who is doing a wonderful job in her role as the First Lady. Her Be Best program, fighting the bullies who torment children, should be an inspiration to the citizens across our country. She should be on the cover of every magazine; Michelle Obama certainly was. Liberal rags have no clue what they are missing, but "We the People" sure do. Thank you, First Lady Melania, you have no idea how many Americans throughout this nation admire and appreciate you! You, Barron, and your entire Trump family have made so many sacrifices for the well-being of America. "We the People" love you all!

I believe that whether CNN, MSNBC, and their cohorts realize it or not, they have and will continue to pay a serious price for their dishonesty and lack of integrity. It is baffling to me that these morons, who claim to be intellectually superior to Trump and his supporters, are so dumb as to not have learned from the 2016 election. Theses fools still believe that "We the People" will come out of our Trump-induced state and see them as the gods that they pretend to be. Instead of getting wiser, they keep doubling down on stupid. It is laughable! These snobby elite dummies are calling us sheeple, when they cannot even figure out *What Happened*, as Hillary Clinton's book is so appropriately titled. (Clue: In her whole book, she never actually guesses what happened.) Even a young child could tell you what happened, but these dingbats refuse to learn. Instead, these Liberals, who look down their noses at the forgotten men and women, just double down and make the same mistakes, over and over again. The mainstream media have proven to be spokespeople without a mind of their own and the integrity to develop a sense of pride in reporting the truth.

In an effort, I have given them the benefit of the doubt, by trying to understand this lack of conscience coming from their fake news outlets. I have concluded that much of their ongoing campaign against President Trump and his supporters is because they cannot let go of their egos and pride. Admitting that President Trump won a fair election in 2016 would be degrading to them because they may have to concede that they were wrong. They are too weak and shallow to list the litany of Trump's accomplishments because that would prove President Trump had become the successful leader that they had said he could never be. Only virtuous and confident individuals can admit when they have made a mistake, and those who do so deserve much honor and respect, I fear that these self-absorbed fake news people do not have the strength to be honest.

On July 3, 2020, as President Trump stood before Mount Rushmore in the Black Hills of Keystone, South Dakota. He gave an impassioned patriotic speech requesting unity throughout our nation in his heartfelt statement, "We believe in equal opportunity, equal justice and equal treatment for citizens of every race, background, religion and creed. Every child of every color, born and unborn, is made in the Holy Image of God."

At the end of that beautiful statement, the entire audience rose for a standing ovation with hooting, hollering, and roaring applause. Our countrymen and women want to embrace each other during these recent sad losses. We reject the evils of racism. Yet two channels over on CNN, their fake news reporters were condemning President Trump with racist narratives, blasting him for visiting the majestic monument, because of the faces of four white leaders, two of which were slave owners. They do not tell you that Barack Obama, Bernie Sanders and Hillary Clinton *all* visited Mount Rushmore, praising it with lovely words regarding its splendor and beauty. CNN's unbelievable hypocrisy never ceases to amaze its viewers! How dare they spew their endless divisive rhetoric in this time of such grieving with the deaths of so many precious black lives.

Fake news is not exclusive to Donald Trump and his family; it also applies to his supporters and those who oppose the views of the Left. We all have become victims of this deceptive reporting.

Whether you are the unwitting believer who forms untrue opinions based on those false narratives or if you are the victim of the lies who is discredited based on unproven allegations, both individuals suffer greatly. These have become much of the reason that our country in such turmoil, and it is so widely divided today. Unfortunately, the culprits in the media will never accept their responsibility in the divisions within our culture; they would rather place the blame at the feet of anyone who does not agree with their ideology or political agenda.

It seems strange to think that news outlets are known for their biases, like Liberal MSNBC or Conservative FOX. News should be impartially offering only the facts; however, even our local TV news shows seem to be anchored by masterful directors of communication, who create your opinion with their condescending tone and facial expressions. Sometimes, they even blatantly offer stories with a twisting of the truth and then direct the commentary by telling you how to think. Keep in mind, conservative points of view are represented by only seven news outlets, compared to the liberal's thirty-two news outlets. And most public places, like airports, bars, and restaurants have left-leaning CNN streaming on a screen. If you do not think that is a form of brainwashing, you are sadly mistaken. My friends, it is a subliminal form of mind control, and we have all been affected by it.

Remember that, there are always at least two sides to every story, but if one of them is a false narrative, you have a big problem. This can be in our relationships with family, friends, coworkers, acquaintances, or instructors, as well as news sources. Can we ever really know where to find the just the facts? I have had to do research for several years to determine where the truth is more likely to be found.

FOX News

I enjoy FOX news for several reasons. Obviously, they do give me likeminded commentary, which supports my feelings as a Conservative. For me, this Conservative perspective has come in handy when trying to articulate my political points of view with others. It also makes sense that we, as audience members, would choose a commentator with whom we can relate. We often develop a respect and trust for that TV host. The trust that I have in FOX News has been not just a gut instinct but based on lots of research. Please believe me when I say I can be critical of a FOX news commentator, if I think that they are overreacting or embellishing the truth; however, I have yet to catch a lie. And I must point out that over the years, a commentator will catch their own mistake, make a retraction, and give a genuine apology.

Another reason that I choose FOX is for the factual stories that you will *not* see on the liberal networks. Remember, fake news applies just as much to the stories that networks omit, as it does to the false narratives that they provoke, it is to inform others in a way which will unite us, with the goal of calming any of their misunderstandings, anger, or fear. Both the stories and the lack of stories can paint a picture that is slanted and even can be terribly deceitful or blatantly wrong. You can destroy a person by pointing out their flaws all day long, as the Left-Wing media have done with President Trump. Or you can create a hero by spreading only their wonderful deeds, as the same networks have done with President Obama. FOX gives both sides to most of their stories in a fair and balanced way, and they offer reports that you will not see anywhere on the mainstream TV shows.

The truth is FOX News has taken a bad beating over the past few decades because of the fake news outlets. It is genius really! If you think about it, the Democrat Party has hijacked the mainstream media, lets them only offer their Left-Wing ideology, and then has them mock anyone who disagrees with that ideology. This strategy of the Left Wing to control the airwaves is intended to control the minds of the people in this country, and it is deliberate. FOX is truthful and powerful, and they know this, too. So the Democrat politicians and their Liberal media friends must destroy FOX News by discrediting and silencing them for opposing their liberal ideology. You just should giggle when if you have an opinion these days, someone will say, "You must be watching *too* much FOX News!"

*****

Now, we can recognize the manipulation and strategies formed against us by the fake news with an agenda. We can seek the truth and notice the lies. We can discern from the journalists, who are honest or who have a hidden motive. We can see with fresh eyes and listen with open minds because we are aware of their deceptive tricks and plans to divide us. These masterful directors of the news stories no longer have power over us.

Alternative news outlets are available on some of the cable networks. OAN is One America Network, CBN is Christian Broadcasting Network, and News Max are all great sources of trusted new reports. YouTube also has news sources such as Just Informed, And We Know, The X22 Report, Woke Societies, Just the News, Jennifer Mac, Black Conservative Patriot, Steel Truth, Lance Wallnau, Judicial Watch, The Patriot Hour, and so many more. You choose who you enjoy and trust to give you the truth and *real* news! And when it comes to a great national newspaper, I love the *Epoch Times*. It is such a wonderful newspaper with great content.

Truth seekers need fact-based resources that they can trust. Be sure to research on your own and find reliable people who have no hidden agendas. And make sure when you spread the word that you are giving *real* news!

CHAPTER 8

War Heroes

Show me the man, and I'll find you the crime.
—Lavrentiy Beria

Their pride and arrogance will be their downfall! There are no justifiable excuses for the horrors that these evildoers have perpetrated on our patriotic heroes and what they have put them through over these past four years. Never would you think that this could happen in America. This is not who we are as a nation; however, this is what we have become. And it is *not* okay!

You wicked ones may think that you are going to get away with this reign of terror, this abuse of power, and this perversion of justice, but you are gravely mistaken. Your haughty nature will be your undoing! Justice is coming for you, and law and order will prevail over our land once again! Watch and wait!

The letters FBI stand for the Federal Bureau of Investigation, and it is said to be known for its "Fidelity, Bravery, and Integrity." Shame on those of you at the top! Shame on you who have enacted these malicious injustices! And shame on those of you who cowardly watched and did nothing! You know who you are, and you are disgusting! You have become, what I now call "The Federal Bullies of Intimidation."

Your demise will be coming soon. And you are not alone, your intelligence agency cronies and political bigwig friends will be going with you. All of you are going to be punished for your lack of honor, your treasonous betrayal of our nation, and your crimes against our war heroes and "We the People." Let me be clear, citizen have recognized that their country has been taken from them by an overbearing shadow government. Americans will not stand back and watch our values and principles be destroyed. We will preserve this nation, one way or another. So call this women's intuition, I truly believe that "if justice is not served through the proper channels soon, these evildoers will see a fury like no other."

And my guess is that "it will not be pretty!"

Drain the Swamp

There's a plot in this country to enslave every man, woman, and child. Before I leave this high and noble office, I intend to expose this plot.
—President John F. Kennedy,
seven days before his assassination

Very wealthy families with tentacles like an octopus have gripped the planet for the past century. These mega-rich dynasties have mocked us while they wield their power enslaving us. These members of a cabal of darkness have no regard for humanity. Their riches could end world hunger in an instant. And yet while they create sham foundations posing as benevolent nonprofit organizations designed to help the poverty-ridden poor, they deceptively launder millions for their own benefit. Although they claim to be compassionate, they are manipulating the masses. Their goal is domination over the entire population with a globalist agenda. These elite rulers have deliberately labeled their plots and schemes as conspiracy theories, but now they have been exposed for all the world to see. The masterful control coming from these uber-affluent families has formed webs of corruption throughout the regimes governing many countries throughout the universe. Trying to break these strongholds has proven to be dangerous, even deadly, and America is witnessing this in our current political environment.

A vindictive politicization of the Obama administration had been running rampant throughout their two terms. While they pontificated about the rule of law and justice, they ignored these standards for their own tribe. With their God complex, they thought that they and their comrades could be above the law. These biased crooks ignored their roles as "servants of the people" and decided to go rogue. Under their authoritarian style regime, the US Constitution and its Bill of Rights only applied to those whom they agreed with politically, thus rendering it meaningless, only to serve half of the country's citizens. It is not revenge that "We the People" are demanding, it is a serious reckoning that we insist upon. As Wyatt Earp said in the movie *Tombstone*, "You called down the Thunder! Well, now you got it! You are finished! The Law is coming, and hell is coming with it!"

The general public thought that they could win a fair election in 2016. Hillary Clinton told us so. She repeatedly snarked, in her superior tone, at Donald Trump that the outcome of the election was to be accepted, no matter what. Trump sensed that there would be voter fraud, and things may have been rigged against him, in the same way Bernie Sanders previously had been cheated. Anyone with half a brain knew that the polls were fake. Did those bozos think that we could not see that Trump was filling stadiums and Hillary could not fill a high school gymnasium? However, an unsuspecting Trump and his supporters never could have imagined the corrupt lengths in which the establishment and the Obama administration would go to destroy him before and even after his victory. And now we know!

Echoing throughout the large Trump rallies, you could hear the pleading chants, "Drain the Swamp! Drain the Swamp!"

"We the People" knew that our problems were more than being ruled by some grossly incompetent morons, who failed to keep their promises. Our government had been corrupted for decades with politicians filling their pockets while picking ours. We knew we needed someone to clean up the whole rotten mess. However, we did not realize how bad the Washington DC Swamp had truly become. The extremely dark and insidious conditions have called for a superhero because the dishonesty has been running so deep. And as we wait for the justice "We the People" deserve, we still cannot be sure that we will get our happy ending!

The swamp creatures were not going to go down without a fight, and they became enraged. They have become physically ugly with their seething green jealousy and extreme anger toward Donald Trump. They have become loathsome and hateful to the forgotten men and women too, for not realizing they, the elites, were supposed to be the ones we admired, not Trump. The growing madness that overcame them was mixed with fear because now that he had become the president, he would have the access to see their dirty little secrets, dark schemes and wicked crimes against Trump's campaign and against humanity. They never counted on Trump winning!

Like rats scurrying when you turn the lights on, the swamp creatures from the Obama administration and the intelligence agencies panicked. They started to leak fake stories to the mainstream media, and they went after and attacked anyone who posed the threat of finding out their dishonest deeds. And then, they made their blatant distain for the American people who voted for Donald Trump apparent when they refused to accept the will of the people by enacting the coup attempt of our duly elected president. As "We the People" voted to save the American Dream, the Deep State plotted to take it away from us forever.

After thirty-three years of service in the military, three-star General Michael Flynn was named National Security Adviser by our newly elected President Donald J. Trump. Flynn knew the National Security Establishment was corrupt, and he planned to clean up and streamline these intelligence agencies. These bad actors knew that he not only stood in their way, but that he would soon see their dishonest activity targeting the Trump campaign. Also, Michael Flynn knew "where the bodies were buried," so to speak, because he had previously worked with the Obama administration. So the Obama holdovers planned to take the general down.

When Michael Flynn was found without a crime, the Federal Bureau of Investigation decided to do whatever it would take to entrap and frame the general, even if it meant that they would have to create a crime. While trying to defend himself, Flynn was bankrupted with legal expenses. He not only lost his home, he was losing his stellar reputation too. Flynn was treated like a traitor. The FBI used threatening tactics, which led to a forced guilty plea by Flynn to spare his family. Ultimately, they destroyed him.

During the same time frame, KT McFarland, who was working as the Deputy National Security Adviser with General Michael Flynn in the Trump administration, was also targeted by the FBI. She tells her story in which these dirty cops tried to set her up with the goal of getting her to implicate President Trump in a crime.

Unbelievable that this could happen in America, a duly elected by the people president could become the victim of a coup to not only remove him from office, but to frame him and his allies for a crime. General Michael Flynn, KT McFarland, and President Donald Trump are our war heroes, along with so many others who got caught up in the crosshairs of the witch hunt!

The Obama administration and his intelligence agencies never had a basis to spy on the Trump campaign, so they invented one. These cheaters never thought that they would get caught. When they could not stop Donald Trump from winning the election in 2016, they perpetrated a fraud on the American people by promoting a Russian collusion theory that never happened. They knew from the beginning there was nothing to this false narrative; however, they intentionally continued to push it. Not just to discredit the new elected president, but to take him out. As their plots and schemes were slowly becoming exposed, they saw their hoax unraveling before their eyes. So like the demons they had become, they publicly doubled down on their lies and deception to give the American people a fictional illusion.

Obama never intended to give Trump a smooth transition of power, he planned to make sure there would be no transition at all. Obama's people continued to work for Obama and his Left-Wing agenda into the Trump administration. They not only undermined and disrespected President Trump's policies, but they deliberately sabotaged his efforts and tried to trip him up every chance they got.

These phonies inside the Trump administration became apparent as President Trump set forth with his promised goal of making America great again. We watched as Trump learned who his allies were and who were resisting his ability to succeed. In a short time, the endless attempts to get him impeached and thrown from office became obvious ploys. As they used their offices to concoct fake crimes against our president so they could investigate and try to set him up, the credibility of these haters was gone, and Trump's counterpunching became justified. However, the severe acts of corruption ran much deeper the superficial bickering, and this will soon go down as the worse scandal in America's history. Obamagate!

The fallout of innocent people who got crushed because they stood in the way of Obama and his officials' plans to destroy President Trump is terribly sad. You may not have a heart for Roger Stone, Paul Manafort, Carter Page, George Papadopoulos, and many more, and to the evildoers, they were merely collateral damage in the war on "We the People," but these men "fell on the sword," so to speak, for the patriotic cause of saving our republic. They got caught in the dark web of the cabal, and they became members of the team of heroes in our patriot movement. Those war heroes have taken the brutal attacks from Obama's officials, who cared nothing about the fact that they would be destroying these American's lives. That is what I can only describe to be, seen as, evil intent! The dirty cops and their conspirators must be held accountable, and I am not talking about a slap on the wrist or a few policy changes. A day of reckoning is coming! This is America, and Americans will stand for nothing less than a maximum punishment for the malicious intent of these rogue swamp creatures from Obama's administration and his intelligence agencies.

*****

It has become apparent to anyone paying attention that we have been at war for these past four years, but if you dig a little deeper, you will find that the enemy has been out to take down our beloved America and replace her entire premise. This war is not just with

Donald Trump, he is simply the guy who got in the way of these very powerful swamp creatures. This overthrowing of America is about the ruling class federal elites, who are embedded bureaucrats and shady politicians that do not want to lose their money, control, and power by giving it back to "We the People." They do not want to end their corrupt ways. By handing the government back to the people, it is over for them, and they will not give up without a fight. As this bunch of bad actors who have been involved in the Obamagate scandal are being called to testify, they blame each other, avoid direct answers, and prolong the process. It is very suspicious that most of these witnesses' standard answer has become "I do not recall."

I feel my standard response become "Bull$#i+!"

Justice being delayed has had its consequences, and it has not been without intentionality. These politically corrupt actors maliciously prolonged the Mueller Investigation for a year and a half after they had confirmed that there had been no collusion between Donald Trump or any of his campaign staffers with the Russians. "We the People" have been duped for several reasons, but one of the most crucial was the outcome of the 2018 election. Losing the majority in the House of Representatives was based on the lies of the Russian collusion hoax. These useless members of the House of Representatives have hindered the ability of our Congress to fulfill its duties, and they have crippled our nation's power to succeed on many critical levels, but the most vicious was their impeachment efforts, which became a huge waste of time and taxpayer dollars. No matter which side of the aisle that you sit, this deception was on the entire American nation and her people, and it has been nothing less than treasonous. What has been labeled as "Justice Delayed" is what I call, "The Theft of the 2018 Election."

Heads must roll!

Republicans do not get a free pass by any means. Do not get me wrong, some of them have been true heroes of our story. Congressmen Devin Nunes, Jim Jordan, Andy Biggs, Mark Meadows (currently, the Chief of Staff for President Trump), Matt Gaetz, John Ratcliffe (currently Director of National Intelligence), and Senators Marsha Blackburn and Ted Cruz, among many others, have been amazingly vocal in supporting President Trump throughout the entire political hit job that they knew was being perpetrated on him and his administration. And some of them have taken great action in the fight against the corruption of the Deep State. However, the RINOs (Republicans in Name Only) have been "Never Trumpers." Some of them, such as John McCain, Mitt Romney, and the Bushes, have openly hated President Trump. Those haters are entrenched establishment elitists whose corruption ties them to the Washington DC Swamp. After Trump's campaign promises to "Drain the Swamp," they had no choice but to align themselves with their swamp creature buddies.

There are also a group of Republicans who have fallen into the category of weak, feckless, and ineffective. The intimidation of the political elitists, who threaten them, causes them to be paralyzed with fear. One can only imagine that those GOP leaders who fall into this scaredy-cat category have possibly had something hanging over their heads, which leaves them powerless, preventing them from fulfilling their duties in representing their constituents. My speculation in watching is that these Republicans who have been complacent by letting the treasonous acts of their political friends take place with no rebuke or accountability may not have done so simply to assist in the theft of the 2018 election and the House of Representatives, but also possibly due to their own corruption and Trump's ability to expose them with the other swamp dwellers.

It is also critical to their treasonous plot of overthrowing the government that they distract the public with one crisis after another to prevent the exposure of their criminal activity. The powerful elite have been creating these diversions and placing the focus on them in the mainstream media, so that citizens are left unaware of their misdeeds. And as the investigators request the material to undercover the truth, evidence and witnesses are being hidden. The den of thieves' plan is to stall, hoping the clock will run out by making sure those who are fact-finding be denied access to any pertinent documents. All the while, the process gets drowned out by overshadowing tragic events that are being flamed by agitators and radicalized activist who incite violence and cause further damage to our nation's ability to succeed. Both sides, the good guys and the bad guys, are scrambling toward the finish line, the 2020 election. If the entrenched establishment of Joe Biden wins the 2020 election, the corruption gets buried in the swamp forever. And if President Donald J. Trump wins, we get four more years to try to save the nation. Who will win the war? The patriots or the swamp creatures?

Daily, we have had many war heroes opening their eyes and becoming aware of the political demons, who have been possessing our world for total domination. We have observed these deceivers long enough, and now we are on to the tricks and schemes of these evildoers. Whether those bad actors call it Globalism, by dressing it up as a generous and tolerant way to exist, we know that in truth, their agendas handicap nations and oppress poor people. And though the Left-Wing Communists curse our desire for Nationalism, presenting it as a selfish form of Fascism or Nazism, patriotic citizens from around the entire world are understanding the importance of protecting their own sovereignty. Country's citizens are becoming aware of the honest facts about how becoming self-sufficient, using policies to grow their own economies, and keeping one's own citizens safe can truly benefit and strengthen them. We are inspiring all nations to put their well-being first so that we all can better help others.

More and more woke to the real reasons for most of the cultural struggles we are undergoing, realizing these diversions must happen as a smoke screen with the stoking of fires to keep all eyes on the escalating flames and off the crimes of the corrupt. Masses of informed persons have grown aware of the brewing plot of the Washington DC Swamp with their tactics of using the Radical Leftists, Marxists, Progressives, and Socialists as pawns. Regardless of race, gender, sexual orientation, or religious background, droves of these woke Americans have united, leaving their labels behind, becoming "As One." These patriotic warriors are politicians, military officers, truth-seeking news reporters, and social media influencers, along with everyday citizens who simply love the USA. They are the brave champions who have joined up to share in the fight to save everything that is their American Dream. These war heroes are in the battle for themselves, their children, and their grandchildren, to preserve our Constitution and our Bill of Rights. Standing strong with one another for the justice, freedom, and liberty that identify us as Americans.

The American Flag

Old Glory was the name given to the Union flag belonging to Captain William Driver. His friends presented him with the flag, which had red, white, and blue stripes with twenty-four stars, for his daring sea rescue of the mutineers and their ship, the *Bounty*. During his travels at sea, Old Glory was proudly flown by the ship-master from Salem, Massachusetts, on the bow of his ship, the *Charles Doggett*. After he retired to Tennessee, he hid the controversial flag inside the quilt on his bed throughout the end of the Civil War. When the Union soldiers conquered the Confederate Army, the Union flag became the American flag. Captain Driver recovered his cherished flag from the quilt and donated it to our government. On February 25, 1862, it was raised to fly over the capital. To this day, Old Glory is part of our nation's history at the Smithsonian Museum in Washington, DC.

The devotion to our flag has always been because of the message for which it stands: a symbol of unity, liberty, and justice for all. After the Civil War, the Union flag was chosen to represent a nation after its horrible battles, with bloodshed and the loss of lives, then ending in the celebration of its victory to shed the sin of slavery from our land. The term Old Glory was used as a nickname to refer to our beautiful flag of the United States of America throughout the following centuries. This national symbol, with its fifty stars representing the entire fifty states, serves as a reminder of challenges we have faced as a country throughout the years and the bond that unites us as one people.

Recently, we have witnessed much disrespect coming from radical dissidents of our beloved American flag. The reasons that they sow discord among our citizenry is contradictory to the significance that our flag represents for our people. While they falsely condemn America for being a racist nation, they kneel at the one symbol that speaks to the fact that we are the opposite. Although racism exists in the hearts of some very bad individuals, on the whole, racism has not been an American trait. We are a country united by that common flag, which was held up in the struggle to end the evils of slavery and the segregation of our people. In dishonoring its symbolism, we further divide the nation and her citizens. To bridge any gap between us, we must stand together as Americans, regardless of race, gender, or creed, and we must pray for healing. We need to realize that respecting our shared American flag promotes our allegiance to our common goals. And it is to our benefit to mutually work to maintain the American Dream of our land, which are the freedoms, liberties, and justice that our founding fathers and other brave men and women throughout the centuries have fought so proudly to secure for us.

For Thoughtful Consideration

Although we have won some serious battles these past few years, this war is not over by a long shot. Do you see the patterns of manufactured events that are being used to distract the general public at convenient times? Do you notice the condescending tones of disapproval or tones of adoration which are used to manipulate your emotions and feelings, depending on the narrative the reporters are spinning? Do you recognize the regurgitated words of the day which are used to saturate your brain to form your opinion to suit their political agenda?

We are becoming so aware of the tricks and schemes of the fake news outlets, that we can feel ourselves recoil in disgust at the lies and deception that have become so common for them and so apparent to us.

CHAPTER 9

California Dreaming

As California goes, so goes the Country.

What the holy hell has happened to California? I was born and raised in the Golden State. However, I just do not recognize it anymore. These days, I rarely desire to go to any of my favorite childhood places. Crowded, polluted, stinky, dirty, littered, unsafe streets are where you left your heart in San Francisco! The homeless crisis has taken over the sunny state, which is not only heartbreaking, but out of control. The drug epidemic has complacently been condoned, while poisoning those who have lost all hope. Tragic fires have ravaged the scenic land, taking many lives and homes of our beloved residents. Sanctuary is available for some, but little safety and justice are available for the law abiding. In my opinion, most of these travesties are due to the radical oppressive mandates, the lack of leadership and the mismanagement of the Democrat politicians with their liberal policies. This can become obvious to anyone who is willing to examine the causes of the destruction of the left-wing-ran cities across our great nation. This debate is worth having, if it means saving the lives of the innocent Americans, who have become victims of these overbearing and devastating policies.

Yes! I am boldly placing the blame on the corrupt and delinquent governing class of this Blue state. While they have enriched themselves, these shady politicians have let the people they are supposed to serve suffer in several ways. My opinion is that the Democrat Party's leadership has let its people down throughout our nation, and we must use Blue-run states and cities as evidence to prove this point. This is easily witnessed simply by opening your eyes to look at the distraught areas like San Francisco, Chicago, New York, Baltimore, Los Angeles, and many other Democrat-ruled cities, which are paralyzed with crime and homelessness. These cities can also be examples of rampant corruption by following the money, waste, and fraud perpetrated on America's taxpayers at the hand of sleazy politicians. In these places, we have watched the middle class and the poor become poorer while the rich get wealthier. Currently in California, our roads and infrastructure are crumbling, while a Smart Train no longer seems very "smart." I challenge you to look at *all* the Blue-governed states and cities to observe their despair and destruction, and then examine the reasons why they are suffering with more crime and poverty than the Red-governed states and cities. For the sake of our people and their communities, we must be honest about what is working, as well as what is not working. Let us look at some highlights.

Blue state policies promote Socialism, which creates a dependency on the government. This gives the citizen a false sense of security because the welfare system gives them a handout and the promise of free healthcare. The recipient of the low costs does not see further into the future to the fact that the government will in return control their destiny, thus enslaving them to their failed policies. This rarely gives the citizen an opportunity to elevate themselves out of poverty to a better station in society. Cnsequently, his oppressive system cripples the middle class by raising their taxes and their costs of living, which furthers the chance of eliminating the middle class altogether. The corrupt politicians love this system because they become wealthier. And best of all for these deceivers, as you become poorer and more dependent on them, they become more powerful. It becomes a vicious greedy cycle with an unfair outcome!

The Red states and cities offer their citizens a hand up rather than a handout. They create opportunity, which leads to the citizen becoming upwardly mobile and promotes self-sufficiency. They know that a strong economy is possible when restrictions and regulations are lifted to advance the small businesses that run their communities. They give their citizens a calming sense of safety and security by enforcing law and order. And Red states also support your right to defend yourself with the Second Amendment. It is interesting that those states have fewer gun-related crimes. Hmmmm? Let us look at that fact.

As a member of the National Rifle Association, I advocate for gun safety and responsibility. The Second Amendment is a guarantee that every citizen has the right to keep and bear arms for their own protection and the protection of their families and their communities. We can debate the pros and cons of the Second Amendment; however, any debate must not be confused with issues that do not apply to law-abiding people. Without the right to defend oneself, citizens run the risk of becoming targets and victims, as opposed to being safe and free.

Another terrifying aspect of Liberalism is the Sanctuary City policies. Yikes! You have to wonder, "Sanctuary for someone from another country, but no sanctuary for our American citizens. Have you lost your freakin' minds?"

I remember the night, July 1, 2015, the beautiful Kate Steinle was murdered. It was a heartbreaking story! Kate and her father were walking along Pier 14 in the Embarcadero, when she was fatally shot by five-time-deported illegal immigrant Jose' Inez Garcia Zarate. He was later acquitted of murder and manslaughter. Did crazy liberal politics give him a free pass? If my husband had accidentally shot a seal, he would most likely serve more time than Zarate. The blatant hypocrisy of the liberal ideology of the Left is maddening, if not intentional. We, the people of common sense, cannot help but ask, "Where is justice for Kate and her family in San Francisco?"

There are endless stories of United States citizens who have been the victims of criminal illegal immigrants. The number one priority of our elected officials should be the lives and well-being of Americans. The angel families who have lost their loved ones to horrendous violence at the hands of these murderers, rapists, and thieves, who are not legally in our country, deserve justice. Where is their sanctuary? You cannot tell me that I am a racist, I know that I am not. Just as we know that these angel families and our president are not racists. We simply want to know that our families and friends are protected and safe. And we expect justice! Come to our country the proper way! Then we can say, "Welcome to America, now obey her laws or leave!"

Log It, Graze It, or Watch It Burn!

During the fire seasons of 2017 through 2019, California has been devastated by wildfires that have blazed 2.9 million acres, and in five of the state's twenty deadliest fires, 131 people were killed. The Woolsey Fire that ravaged Los Angeles and Ventura Counties, November 8 through 21 in 2018, killed three civilians and injured five people, three of which were firefighters. This fire alone burned 96,949 acres, destroyed 1,643 buildings, and damaged iconic properties such as the Reagan Ranch and movie sets, such as that of the hit series *MASH*. During that same time frame, the camp fire that devastated Butte County was even worse. It claimed the lives of 85 civilians, injuring 12 civilians and 5 firefighters. This fire destroyed 18, 804 buildings and burned through 153,336 acres. And this firestorm took nearly the entire town of Paradise and the community of Concow. These two fires costs were a total of 22.5 billion dollars. It was during these horrific disasters that President Trump wrote a warning to California, "There is no reason for these massive, deadly, and costly forest fires in California except that forest management is so poor. Billions of dollars are given each year, with so many lives lost, all because of gross mismanagement of the forests. Remedy now, or no more Fed payments!"

As he said during his campaign in September of 2018, Governor Gavin Newsom blames climate change for our catastrophic fires, "The science is clear, increased fire threat due to climate change is becoming a fact of life in our state. Drier, longer summers combined with unpredictable wet winters have created dangerous fire conditions."

It is up for debate! Let us think fairly regarding both, the president's and the governor's, sides of this issue. Responsibility can be taken on many sides of this argument. And let us face it, there is a lot of blame to go around. For instance, California's primary energy distributor Pacific Gas & Electric has taken much of the hits, in both the blame game and financial department, in owning their part in the heartbreaking events. Unfortunately, they appear to be more of a scapegoat for those who want monetary compensation, but we know that they are not entirely at fault for California's ruin.

Another factor is while environmentalists will tell you that global warming is responsible for the widespread fire devastation that has plagued California for the past five or more years, we can definitely place some of the blame on Mother Nature; however, most of the cause is due to policies the environmentalist groups have inspired. Let us take for example, the restrictions that have been made because of the environmentalist agenda to fight for the lives of the spotted owl. In the early '90s, the logging industry became the target of those wishing to protect the spotted owl by setting forward to place more restraints on the ability to harvest timber. Expecting the owls to flourish was their intended goal; instead, the numbers of owls continued declining. So while the harvesting of trees was limited, the fire danger grew. You see, a forest will become thick with trees and brush which grow wild or die, so you must manage it properly. Thus, if loggers had been allowed to cut more trees, all these fires would not be happening to this extent. Log it, graze it, or watch it burn!

My husband, Tom, spent twenty-two years as a heavy fire equipment operator for Cal Fire. Together, we decided that he should retire in July of 2018. The prior three years of his tenure fighting fires up and down California had become increasingly dangerous. I asked him what he felt contributed to the steady inability to get control of these wildfires, to the point where they had overtaken towns and even cities. Poor leadership is one of many issues because of officials, like Newsom, who ignore and deny the root of the problem. When the mismanagement and neglect of our forests exists, the fires become too strong to contain, spreading them to neighboring communities. As the population of California has been booming, homes are being pushed further and further to the outskirts of towns, butting some right into the brushy areas. Residents are not allowed the opportunity for control burns in the way they freely could exercise that task in years past, which gave landowners less fuel surrounding their properties. And add on top of that, property owners are hit with high state fees that make it unaffordable to get permits. During this most recent Walbridge Fire, which was frighteningly close to our home in Sonoma County, Cal Fire did not have enough firefighters or equipment to send to our little community. Our Parmeter family, friends, and neighbors joined forces to save our small town and surrounding areas. I am not exaggerating when I say they were all local heroes left on their own to stop the devastating fire as it ripped up the canyons and over the mountains. This exemplifies what the forgotten men and women of America do when they are left to fend for themselves!

I admire and appreciate the views of environmentalists who have respect for nature, our land, water, and some parts of life. However, the liberal policies they cling to make us suffer in so many other ways. As we fear the fires that have been wildly raging all around the state, California's environment and people are choking with smoke and ash. Not only does this make our elderly and those with lung illnesses suffer terribly, the ash and fire retardant have polluted our creeks, streams, and rivers. Citizens are forced to stay in their homes because the air quality is four times worse than that of Beijing or New Delhi. Unless you are not so lucky and live in an area which is being threatened by fire. Those citizens have been subject to evacuations which have become mandatory, displacing tens of thousands of residents. As we pack up our children and animals with all their belongings, we also gather every precious, sentimental, and valuable item we own, and we leave our properties behind, worried that we may not have a home to return to. On the morning he headed out to fight the blazing fires with his family, my husband kissed me good-bye, turned to leave, then he looked back and whispered, "It is only mid-August, so do not plan on unpacking until mid-November."

CALIFORNIA DREAMING

Homeless Crisis and Drug Epidemic

Poisonous needles and human feces are lying at their feet, as tourists with little children walk through the streets of San Francisco. The smells of urine and waste fill the air. The drug addicts and homeless chatter to themselves or hurl crazy talk at passersby, who must step around or over them. Fear may grip your children, as they edge closer to you and cling a bit tighter to your hand. You must pay better attention to those around you, rather than enjoy the scenery, because you or your loved ones run the risk of being shoved, knocked over, or even accosted. Panhandlers are everywhere, and they can be quite intimidating.

It would be unfair to blame those who have become abandoned by the ruling class of our inner cities. Some are in dire need of medical attention, some have befallen tough times, and some by no fault of their own have simply been lost in the system that was supposed to take care of them. While prices rise and incomes do not, everyday men and women cannot survive in the big cities. These Democrat-run metropolitan areas have become places where elite establishments cater to the rich and reject the common folks. Middle-class Americans move to the suburbs, and the poor have nowhere to go but the streets. Poverty and despair are being acceptable and ignored. After the campaigning is over, the greedy politicians leave their constituency with broken promises. The Nancy Pelosis and Gavin Newsoms of the world line their pockets with taxpayer dollars, then forget about the problems facing the common people and districts they are elected to manage.

San Francisco is not the only Blue city that has been desecrated, Los Angeles, Portland, and list is shameful. You can tell the everyday men and women that these problems have nothing to do with Liberal policies; however, common sense tells us otherwise. President Trump has offered up real solutions with HUD Secretary Ben Carson, in December 2018 establishing a council which pledged to support the administration's efforts to provide for urban and economically challenged areas with public and private investors. These opportunity zones are to benefit underprivileged rural, urban, suburban, and tribal communities with affordable housing and incentive programs. Among the goals of this council are the programs of reentry for those who have served their prison terms into society and the mentorship of at-risk youth. For more information regarding their many services to low-income areas, you can visit www.OpportunityZones.gov.

Solutions coming from our Federal government must be met with a positive response from the local and state leaders, for them to succeed. And this includes the need for the Federal leaders to work together to effectively benefit the entire nation. As an example, US Senator Tim Scott (R-SC) with his colleagues Senators Todd Young (R-IN), Pat Roberts (R-KS), Marsha Blackburn (R-TN), Ben Sasse (R-NE), Steve Daines (R-MT), Martha McSally (R-AZ), James Lankford (R-OK), and Bill Cassidy (R-LA) presented Congress with a relief package for opportunity zones in the wake of the COVID-19 virus shutdown; however, the Democratic leaders rejected it. If you take the time to read the highlights of Scott's team's proposal, it will make you realize that compassion for humanity was lost when the Liberal politicians voted against it.

Below are the ten requests outlined in the letter directed to the US Treasury Department from Scott and his Republican team:

1. Treasury and the Internal Revenue Service should provide relief to the 180-day investment period for a taxpayer's sale or exchange of capital gain property to be contributed to a Qualified Opportunity Fund under section 26 U.S.C. § 1400Z–2(a)(1)(A). This period should be extended by three months for all 180-day investment periods provided in the implementing regulations and underlying statute with respect to capital gains for which the 180-day period would end on or after March 13, 2020, and on or before December 31, 2020.

2. Treasury and the Internal Revenue Service should provide that the failure of a Qualified Opportunity Fund to meet the required 90 percent investment standard for any testing date taking place during the period beginning on March 13, 2020, and ending on July 15, 2020, automatically meets the standard for reasonable cause and subse-

quently avoids penalties under 26 U.S.C. § 1400Z-2(f) (3). Further, with respect to any failure of the 90 percent asset test by a Qualified Opportunity Fund taking place after July 15, 2020, and before January 1, 2021, where the fund can sufficiently demonstrate that the failure is a result of the effects of the COVID-19 pandemic, reasonable cause should be established and the penalties should not apply. Treasury and the Internal Revenue Service should also consider providing an additional 180 days for Qualified Opportunity Funds to disregard recently contributed property beyond the existing six-month period for the purposes of meeting the 90 percent asset test where appropriate throughout 2020.

3. Treasury and the Internal Revenue Service should make clear that the 24-month extension of the working capital safe harbor available to Qualified Opportunity Zone Businesses located within a federally declared disaster area pursuant to Treas. Reg. § 1.1400Z2(d)-1(d)(3)(v), automatically applies to all Qualified Opportunity Businesses nationwide under the President's Stafford Act Emergency Declaration for the COVID-19 pandemic. This period should begin on March 13, 2020, and extend until the earlier of the end of the Emergency Declaration or the period requested by the taxpayer and available under Treas. Reg. § 1.1400Z2(d)-1(d)(3)(v). This extension should also apply to the maximum 62-month period for working capital safe harbors, for a total of 86 months, where appropriate.

4. Treasury and the Internal Revenue Service should make clear that the 12-month extension available to Qualified Opportunity Funds to reinvest proceeds from the sale, disposition, or return of capital from Qualified Opportunity Zone property when reinvestment plans are delayed due to a federally declared disaster pursuant to Treas. Reg. § 1.1400Z2(f)-1(b)(2), automatically applies to all Qualified Opportunity Funds nationwide under the President's Stafford Act Emergency Declaration for the COVID-19

pandemic. This period should begin on March 13, 2020, and extend for the maximum 12-month period thereafter.

5. Treasury and the Internal Revenue Service should also ensure that redemptions of investment capital in excess of an entity's basis in a Qualified Opportunity Fund due to the effects of COVID-19 should automatically be considered an inclusion event pursuant to Treas. Reg. § 1.1400Z2(c)-1(b)(1)(v). This treatment should be provided throughout the duration of the President's Stafford Act Emergency Declaration for the COVID-19 pandemic, beginning on March 13, 2020.

6. Treasury and the Internal Revenue Service should also use its authority under 26 U.S.C. § 7508A(a) to provide a 12-month extension to the 30-month substantial improvement period allotted for Qualified Opportunity Zone property under 26 U.S.C. § 1400Z-2(d)(2)(D)(ii) that is undergoing or expected to begin or complete its substantial improvement period at any point during 2020, for a total of 42 months.

7. Treasury and the Internal Revenue Service should also make clear that Qualified Opportunity Zone Businesses using the regulatory safe harbor that takes into account the location in which services are performed for the purpose of satisfying the requirement that 50 percent of the business' gross income be derived from their active business conduct in the Qualified Opportunity Zone does not wrongfully punish employees who may be teleworking outside of their normal working locations within an Opportunity Zone due to the circumstances of the COVID-19 pandemic.

8. Similarly, Treasury and the Internal Revenue Service should also provide relief to the requirement that a substantial portion—defined as 40 percent—of a Qualified Opportunity Zone Business' intangible property be used in its active conduct within an Opportunity Zone. Specifically, the use of such intangible property outside of its normal utilization location within a Qualified

Opportunity Zone during the conduct of such a business for the purpose of generating gross income as a result of the COVID-19 pandemic should be considered to have been used within a Qualified Opportunity Zone, provided that such use takes place during the period in which the President's Emergency Declaration under the Stafford Act for COVID-19 is in effect. Given the overwhelming amount of Americans working remotely during this crisis, this guidance would prevent the punishment of such employers for taking the necessary steps to comply with COVID-19 ordinances and promote the health and safety of our communities. Likewise, where a Qualified Opportunity Zone Business can sufficiently demonstrate that its failure to meet the 70 percent tangible property test in 2020 is due to delays caused by the COVID-19 pandemic, Treasury and the Internal Revenue Service should give such entities additional consideration when deliberating whether a reasonable cause exception applies.

9. In addition, we ask that you consider providing Qualified Opportunity Funds with an additional cure period equal to six months for each trade or business that causes a fund to fail the 90 percent asset test if the trade or business can demonstrate that its loss of qualification was caused or facilitated by the COVID-19 pandemic.

10. Lastly, any guidance provided with respect to the above requests should include strong anti-abuse language and require those taking advantage of the liberalized timelines to document the facts and circumstances to substantiate that their fund or business merits the beneficial treatment where appropriate and without creating undue or unnecessary burdens. We also recognize that the respective IRS forms and systems may need to be updated in order to facilitate the efficient and accurate enforcement of these recommendations and ensure that entities using these extensions are able to properly indicate such use.

It is obvious that those politicians who cannot reach across the aisle to work with their fellow elected officials to make decisions that will better the lives of their constituents must be voted out of office to make way for a proactive group of leaders who truly care about the people.

There has been a mass exodus of residents from the states which are primarily ruled by Democrat leaders. These people are packing up their lives and moving to the Republican-ran states and cities. The way of life is fairer in those places, the population is down, and the crime rates are lower. Taxes are less burdensome, and freedoms are available to the law-abiding citizens, as opposed to the sanctuary of illegals. "We the People" are being pushed out of our homes to find peace and prosperity elsewhere. The funniest thing I hear is when my Democrat friends say that they are moving, too. Please do not follow the Patriots to a conservative utopia, because as much as we love you, we need you to either change your vote to Red or move somewhere Blue.

The waging cultural war that has been unleashed by Antifa and Black Lives Matter radicalized activists is a perfect representation of the dire differences between the current Democrat Party and the Republican Party. Utilizing the tragic event of the death of George Floyd at the hands of an evil police officer for their political benefit has been beyond contemptible. Every one of us were united across America by the same emotion of disgust and anger when we saw the horrific video of Floyd's death, yet the peaceful protesters' message was lost by a group of well-paid anarchists who provoked violence, destruction, looting, and rioting. Innocent victims were terrorized, injured, and murdered. Innocent victims lost their businesses and livelihoods. Wealthy elitists, like puppet masters behind the scenes, paid for weapons and thugs to attack blameless bystanders and destroy property. These ruling class monsters have tortured our nation with the tactics of a trauma-based form of mind control and their minions enforce its principles. If you do not bend the knee and conform to their demands, they will tighten their grip. Tighter and tighter! You must believe what you are told to believe or the trauma increases until you give in to their group think. As they squeeze tighter, making you conform to their bull$#*+," they push more bull$#i+ down your throat. And even though you know its bull$#i+, you must speak no evil about their bull$#i+. Sick of the bull$#i+" yet?

This insurgency of Marxist type rebels has been thrust upon American soil, and it has become like a deadly cancer attacking us from within. The powerful global elitists have used us by pitting us against one another, while they have been plotting the destruction of the United States of America's sovereignty to further a New World Order. "We the People" have two clear and extremely different choices in the upcoming election of 2020. Are you willing to give up your American Dream? The Left wants power and control. The Right wants to preserve the rights and freedoms in the hands of the people. The Left wishes to destroy our Constitution and remove our history. The Right wants to honor our Constitution and to guard our history. The Left is anti-God and the Right is pro-God. Apparently, the Left wants to defund the police and ICE. The Right is for law and order. They are coming for your vote. They are pandering to you on bended knee, begging for your vote. The choices are crystal clear, my friends! Choose wisely!

The Democrat Party is no longer the party of JFK. They are no longer the working man's party. They have become radicalized by masterful deceivers. However, some of them are very good people who have not realized that they have been tricked. They have become extremely angry, based on lies and schemes. But beware of the very bad people pulling their strings! The only way to get out of this vicious cycle of resistance and hate is to turn a light on the darkness with truth and end the manipulation coming from those who are entrenched in the corruption of our government. It is their lust for power and greed that keeps us enslaved, divided, weak, and poor. Remember though, there is a lot of cleansing to be done on both sides of the aisle. Because both political parties, Republican and Democrat, have establishment elitists that must be voted out of office. Vote wisely!

Patriots are compassionate! We love our people and our country! We want prosperity, justice, and safety for all citizens! The

Democrat leader's policies that we see being implemented in the Blue states and cities are creating poverty, injustice, and violence. While Socialism is being falsely taught to be a loving and generous way to run a country, we can witness its truth of chaos and despair. Under the Liberal agenda, people have no hope of climbing any ladders of success; instead, they are held to a stagnant place with no hope of upward mobility. Open your eyes, look at these geographical areas that are under one party of Democrat rulers, at a state and local level. They have been in control for far too long, and silent observers have cringed, as we have watched the lack of leadership. Let us find strong leaders who care about their constituents more than power and their pocketbooks!

For Thoughtful Consideration

How are Baltimore, Chicago, Seattle, Los Angeles, New York, Detroit, Portland, and San Francisco looking to you today? For over a decade, those are cities in states that have been run by Democrat mayors and governors, and most of their local legislators are liberal too. Do you believe they have gotten the leadership they have needed? What do you think has contributed to their rise in homelessness, filth, poverty, and crime?

Is it apparent to you that the welfare system is designed in such a way that the recipient's dependency on governmental subsidies does more to enslave them than to uplift them? Do the failed policies of the government contribute to this form of enslavement? Do you recognize the manipulation being perpetrated on the lower-income citizens to keep them controlled by the ruling class? If this is an intentional process to dominate those who are less fortunate, would you agree that the welfare system has become a political tool in which lofty elites try to sway citizens, hindering their ability to vote for the things that will truly benefit them and their communities? Should candidates who use a form of bribery while on the campaign trail be held accountable for their lack of action in keeping their promises?

How do you think we can overcome these repetitive problems which have led to mass poverty within our nation?

CALIFORNIA DREAMING

Homelessness is an ongoing crisis which has gotten worse and will continue to get even worse if we do not select the right leaders. Blue cities and states have been mismanaged by delinquent leaders for far too long! It is time for us to hold our leaders accountable and to choose our governing class wisely. But most importantly, it is time to vote for civil servants who will make crucial changes with positive impacts that are visible and can be felt. If we cannot see and feel the benefits, then they are not worth having. Provided that we maintain our Republic, the power is in our voting and the choices we make with those votes. Our rulers know this and that is why they will make We the People all kinds of elaborate promises. We must not let candidates for office continue to fool us, then abandon us with no rewarding solutions. Our vote matters!

CHAPTER 10

Defending the President

*I may not be Donald Trump now, but just you
wait; if I don't make it, my children will.*
—Barack Obama in April 1991

I f you hate Donald Trump, you will probably hate this chapter. If you hate Donald Trump, then you are a hater. Or do we get to pick and choose when we are lovers and when we are haters? When is it acceptable to saturate yourself in hating and loathing a person daily? You may claim to be a *lover* but hate makes you a *hater!* Your statement of "Love trumps hate" becomes meaningless while you parade around spewing your hatred. If you have decided to hate Donald Trump, then you have made that agreement with yourself, and this chapter will not convince you to love him. Instead, you will see everything in this chapter with an excuse. "But he said this, so I know he is this" or "But he did this, so I know he is that." My friends, if our character is determined by a few isolated instances, we all would either be one extreme or the other. So do not expect to change your feelings about President Trump after reading this chapter, unless you have an open heart and would like to have a president that you can accept. At the very least, consider from a selfish standpoint how nice it would be to become a *lover* and not a *hater.*

Reading the quote above from Barack Obama has got to make you wonder, why do so many politicians admire their opponents until they get in the same arena together? Donald Trump was well loved until he decided to run for political office. He was thought of as an incredibly successful businessman and an entertaining reality TV star. Hollywood stars and professional athletes could be seen enjoying The Donald's company until it was not cool any longer. Unless they were strong enough to have their own opinions, like Kanye West. Did you know that Donald Trump has always been extremely generous and known for his heart of gold?

There are so many stories that brilliantly sum up the Donald Trump that we have known for the last half of a century. We all have had the opportunity to observe this man in the public's eye for decades. He had never been known in a negative way until June 16, 2015, the day he descended from the elevator at Trump Tower to announce that he would be running for president of the United States of America.

You do not have to love Donald Trump or even like him. And if you prefer to hate him, you can live in that hate. However, my intention is for you to be objective and understand much of what you have heard about our president is based on other people's hatred and desire to influence your opinion. Keep in mind that when you make an agreement with yourself about someone or something, you will rarely be strong enough to change your opinion because of your overwhelming desire to be right. However, we all can agree that feeling love is always sweeter than feeling hate.

Let us examine the truth about The Donald. He lives a relatively clean lifestyle, he does not drink alcohol, smoke, or take drugs. He is a wonderful father and role model, to his five children who have turned out to be respectable, hardworking human beings. He is a successful businessman who has offered to share his knowledge with others. And he generously donates his time, resources, and money to help others in need.

Random Acts of Kindness

Some of the stories of charitable contributions that Donald Trump has lovingly made over the last several decades may not be found in the media today; however, I have highlighted them below. For more thorough details, you can Google and read these facts.

At sixty-six years of age, Annabel Hill was facing the loss of her family farm. The recent widow desperately pleaded for help by reaching out to the media. In 1986, when Trump saw the story, it touched his heart, and he compassionately made calls to intervene with the sale and gifted Annabel the money that prevented the foreclosure.

A three-year-old boy with a rare illness, Andrew Ten needed to travel from Los Angeles to New York to receive much needed medical treatment in 1988. His family was refused access to a commercial flight because of his many pieces of therapeutic equipment. The Orthodox Jewish family contacted Donald Trump to see if he could help. Without pause, Trump sent his personal crew and plane, which flew the child and his family across the country to the Schneider Children's Hospital of Long Island Jewish Medical Center.

Donald Trump also sent his private plane and crew to make a couple trips from North Carolina to Miami to safely return two hundred Gulf War Marines, who proudly served in Operation Desert Storm to their homes. In 1991, these Marines had been stranded and delayed at Camp Lejune, while waiting to get back to their families.

When a story would touch Donald Trump's heart, he often tried to be thoughtful and generous in any way possible. In 2000, a little girl appeared on *The Maury Povich Show*. Meghan had brittle bone disease, and she had an amazing spirit of optimism. Donald contacted Maury, and on a follow-up show, Povich presented Meghan and her mother with a check from Mr. Trump saying, "We're not talking about chump change here."

You may remember that Jennifer Hudson's mother and brother were brutally murdered in 2008. Donald Trump not only footed the bills to house Jennifer and some of her family members at his International Hotel and Tower in Chicago, but he also paid for them to have security detail to keep them safe.

In 2013, a woman was spotted standing at the edge of a bridge looking down at the traffic below. A New York bus driver Darnell Barton bravely stopped his bus, got out, and saved the woman's life by putting his arm around her and convincing her not to jump. Donald Trump was moved by the heroic story, so he sent Darnell a check for $10,000 as a reward.

In 2014, when he heard that President Barack Obama did not attempt to get Marine Sgt. Andrew Tahmooressi home, after spending seven months in a Mexican jail for accidentally crossing over the Mexico border, Donald Trump sent the Marine sergeant $25,000 to help get him settled back in the USA.

Donald Trump, in his letter to former Miss Wisconsin USA Melissa Consin Young, says, "To the bravest woman I know." Melissa had been struggling with an incurable illness, and she found herself blessed by Trump and his organizations, which provided her Mexican American son a full scholarship to college. Her love for our president became evident at a 2016 Trump rally where she thanked him, with tears streaming down her face.

I have gotten to know Lynne Patton, as part of the Women for Trump Campaign. You can see her true love for President Trump and his family. Lynne is a black woman who has been an executive for the Trump Organization for many years. She can be seen in an impassioned video offering her tearful testimony of her struggles with substance abuse and addiction for years while being supported by the loyal Trump family. She has spent much of her time, over these past several years, defending her boss against the constant barrage of accusations that he is a racist. Lynne knows nothing could be further from the truth!

*****

Those of us who know the real Donald know that he is not a racist, bigot, or any of the horrible names his haters label him with. He is genuine, funny, and imperfect like the rest of us, but he is never hateful. His daughter, Ivanka Trump, said it best, "My dad is color-blind and gender neutral."

President Trump says, "Every day, I wake up determined to deliver a better life for the people across this nation that have been neglected, ignored, and abandoned. I have visited the laid-off factory workers and the communities crushed by our horrible and unfair trade deals. These are the forgotten men and women of our country."

Donald Trump got us, and he still gets us, when nobody else bothers to care. We are the Trump supporters who will fight for this president because we know that he is fighting for us. He is taking beatings from fellow politicians and the mainstream media daily. They have bludgeoned him with their endless attacks. And regardless, he keeps on fighting for us. So we will keep on fighting for him.

In the same way President Trump understands his supporters, we have understood him. I have watched him carefully for the past five years and I have gotten to know him well. The Donald is engaging, animated, and hilarious. As President Trump, he is a caring man and he listens intently to both his constituency and his political advisors. As Businessman Trump, he knows how to negotiate and reciprocate to get the best deals possible. As a father and husband, he is devoted to his family, who love him deeply. When he sees an injustice, he reacts, and he is fiercely loyal. And Trump is a counterpuncher! I have rarely seen him attack anyone who has not struck him, his family, or "We the People" first. When he retaliates, I defend him from the haters who label him with dishonorable names. I have enjoyed winning any debate by asking, "Can you name one person who did not speak disrespectfully about Trump before he fought back?"

I have not had one person answer that question. Those conversations about Donald Trump have not ended with an innocent victim who had been bullied by him first. It amazes me how hard Trump's haters try to rationalize their accusations against him. And if you tell them that a nasty story about the president has been debunked, they will vehemently argue as if they will somehow get a different outcome. It is almost as if they are praying he will become the monster they want him to be so passionately. They themselves become flustered and often simply grunt some obscenity toward me or Trump, which makes them appear to be the bullies they claim Trump to be. Regardless, I am faithful that one day soon, they will realize that their hate has been blinded by masterful deceivers. Until then, my standard prayer has become "Bless them, Lord, for they know not what they do."

The other statement we hear often is that "Trump lies."

His haters claim absurd numbers of lies, like a "Bazillion!" It is outrageous! I can buy that he might have made a few slip ups here or there and even exaggerated. However, the Donald Trump that I know is blatantly honest to the point of getting himself into trouble. So once again, I ask his accusers, "Name three lies that he has told."

Then comes their "deer in the headlights" blank stare. And I ask, "Okay, well, just give me one?"

Sometimes, they will come up with some lie that they have been fed or a twisting of some of Trump's words. However, I find it ridiculous that, Radical Liberals simply *need* something to substantiate their claims of Trump's incompetence. That *need* is like a drug to them, but it comes off as petty. I never liked Barack Obama for eight years, and I could give you long lists of the reasons why, but I did not. Instead, I just "put on my big girl panties" and made the best of it. Always reminding myself of the rule that Thumper's mother always gave, "If you don't have anything nice to say, don't say anything at all."

I remember at one of Trump's rallies, he stepped up to the podium and said, "I can be presidential, but that is boring, you don't want that guy." He is right, we do not want boring, we want real. This president makes us laugh, and he laughs with us, not at us like the political and Hollywood elite. He is not one of those snobby elites, and we thank God that he is not. Through it all, the bad days and the good days, Donald Trump has proven that when he needs to be, he can be very presidential indeed.

As for the snooty elites, it does amaze me that this self-proclaimed intelligent group of people can be so blatantly stupid. Obviously, they are not aware that we see that they are nothing but a bunch of dummies. After their epic failings, do they really think that they can fool us with their regurgitated rhetoric? Have they not figured out that we have not and we will not fall for their tricks and schemes? How wrong do they have to be and for how long?

If the definition of insanity is doing the same thing over and over and expecting different results, then does it suggest, these morons in the mainstream media, politicians, and celebrities who over and over undermine and demean our president in the hopes of swaying our opinions of him but fail to see their desired result, themselves are not an intelligent group. These greedy power-mongering Liberal elites, whose smug narcissism is rooting in hatred and jealousy of a man that they cannot defeat, are left seething with anger and rage. Our country and her people have become the innocent victims of their anger and rage because they have broken our unity and weakened our prosperity.

On the other hand, President Donald J. Trump has lifted our nation up with a litany of accomplishments because of his America First agenda. He has managed to win on almost every level with of his Conservative policies. We saw President Trump end burdensome regulations and lower taxes to strengthen our economy to become the envy of the world. He has been in the process of building the wall at our southern border for national security. And Donald Trump is a leader who does not play favorites. Everyone has been given more opportunities under his administration. As Dr. Ben Carson shares the analogy, he says, "President Trump lifts all the boats, as the tide rises under his leadership."

As President Trump tries his best to fulfill all his campaign promises and fights diligently for us, he is being constantly harassed by establishment swamp creatures, media zombies, and foreign adversaries. Does this warrior do it for money? No! He is a man who generously donates his $400,000 presidential paycheck each year to worthy American charities. Does this leader do it for love? Yes! He is a man who loves his family and his country, and he gives 100 percent to putting America First! And so, because President Trump has proven himself, over and over, I have truly come to love this president, and I will defend him unapologetically!

*****

DEFENDING THE PRESIDENT

President Trump has proven to be very successful at keeping his campaign promises. Trump's achievements are exceedingly far beyond any past presidential record. He has appointed to fill the vacant positions in the US civil courts with hundreds of judges, including two Supreme Court justices, and as promised, he chose those who would adhere to the guidelines of the Constitution. He has reduced our taxes and ended burdensome regulations for businesses. As he avoids unwarranted wars, he has been rebuilding our United States military, for the sake of our national security. And he gave the largest military pay raise in nearly a decade. Please bear with me because it gets even better!

On October 12, 2018, the *Washington Examiner*'s article by Paul Bedard was titled, "Trump's List: 289 Accomplishments in Just 20 Months, 'relentless' promise-keeping." Wow! What a victory for America! And yet you have never heard any of this in the mainstream media. Although I will simply touch upon some of the highlights, keep in mind that this was just the start the promises fulfilled and Trump's projection of "winning, winning, winning!"

When naysayers provoke you, stand firm in defending President Trump's record of accomplishments. Many are mentioned throughout this book, and below, I have compiled a random sampling of other victories. However, always remember that these are only of some of his triumphs for the United States and her people. And as Trump says, "The best is yet to come!"

Since the 2016 election, over four million new jobs have been created. More Americans are employed now than ever before in our history. Jobless claims are at lowest level in nearly five decades. And the economy has achieved the longest positive job-growth streak on record. Women's unemployment rate is at lowest in nearly sixty-five years. African American, Hispanic American, and Asian American unemployment rates have all reached record lows, too. Also, youth unemployment reached its lowest level in more than fifty years, and veterans' unemployment rate hit its lowest level in nearly two decades. And, the unemployment rate for Americans without a high school diploma reached a record low and so did the rate for disabled

Americans. All Americans are gifted because of our businessman president, who is busy reversing the stagnant policies of the past.

Small business optimism has hit historic highs, with the highest percentage ever. Ninety-five percent of US manufacturers are enthusiastic about their future. The small business optimism index broke a thirty-five-year-old record, and in a small business confidence survey for the third quarter of 2018, it matched its all-time high. And manufacturers are coming back to America because they are more confident than ever. It was President Obama who got rid of a lot of our manufacturing jobs when he shipped them to China. Because of that decision, it brought the GDP down to 1.8 percent during his time in office. When Candidate Trump promised to bring jobs back and raise the GDP, Obama smugly responded in disbelief, "Well, what, how exactly are you going to do that? What magic wand do you have?"

President Trump used the magic wand of a businessman who knew how to enrich our country and her people with his deal-making mentality. Trump passed the Congressional Review Act to massively deregulate the burdensome rules restricting the ability for businesses to produce and manufacture in America. This immediately opened the production of steel, aluminum, oil, and natural gas, which by coming back, has made America energy independent. Trump also signed the legislation to end the costly and destructive provisions of Dodd-Frank, giving relief to community banks, regional banks and credit unions. Also, by taking away strict regulations, Trump was able to achieve a long-term regulatory net cost savings of more than 8 billion dollars for federal agencies.

With the businesses flourishing, middle-class wages increased. Household incomes rose at their fastest rate since the recession of 2009 under Barack Obama. Trump rewarded Americans with the biggest tax cuts and reforms in our countries history by signing the Tax Cuts and Jobs Act into law. Thanks to the tax cuts, more than 6 million American workers have received higher pay, bonuses, and other benefits. Homeownership among Hispanics has been at the highest rate in nearly a decade. Poverty rates for African Americans and Hispanic Americans have reached their lowest levels ever recorded. And over

3.9 million Americans have been lifted off food stamps since Trump took office. He established opportunity zones to promote investment in poor communities. And he increased the exemption for the death tax to help save families, especially those with farms and small business. We see the "trickle-down effect" of success for all Americans!

As Candidate Trump promised, he would crack down on crime, drugs, and be our law and order" president. He has followed through by enforcing stronger Border Security and Immigration Laws. His promise of a southern border wall started, and construction has been underway; thus far, approximately two hundred miles have been completed. In the fiscal year of 2017, there was an 83 percent increase in the arrests of MS-13 gang members. Under his leadership, Trump's Department of Homeland Security has been fighting to stop the illegal drugs pouring into our country at our southern border. To combat the war on drugs, President Trump signed the Interdict Act into law, enhancing efforts to detect and intercept synthetic opioids. Trump's Department of Justice also secured indictments, for the first time, against Chinese fentanyl manufacturers. And the Department of Justice launched their Joint Criminal Opioid Darknet Enforcement Team, in order to stop online illegal opioid sales.

Under Trump administration, after ending the disastrous Iran Deal of Obama, Mike Pompeo placed new sanctions on Iran. This new policy includes nuclear and missile programs. Renegotiating with Iran and implementing stricter guidelines were in keeping with one of the promises made by President Trump on his 2016 campaign trail.

President Trump's administration has managed to make trade deals like no other presidential administration in the history of our nation. His "Art of the Deal" techniques have come in handy, while he has negotiated and renegotiated stronger trade deals by making them fair and reciprocal policies for the United States. Trump withdrew from the job-killing Trans-Pacific Partnership. Trump's team tackled a new North American Trade Agreement; this new deal is now called the US-Mexico-Canada Agreement, also known as USMCA. Trump has said the revised agreement will have "the most advanced protections for the American workers that has ever been developed."

Also, let us not forget that Trump confronted China on their unfair trade practices, after decades of our government letting China take advantage of us, and they made significant changes to balance the benefits. Trump has done more for our American farmers because of these masterful trade deals that reward them greatly.

Trump's plans for repealing and replacing the costly and ineffective Obamacare health plan has been a long process, held back by Congress. However, Trump has successfully been able to make significant changes that benefit all Americans. First, Trump cut Obamacare's burdensome individual mandate penalty. He signed an executive order to guarantee that religious institutions will not have to choose between violating their religious beliefs or shutting their doors because of Obamacare's contraceptive mandate. Trump also overturned the Obama administration's midnight regulation, which prohibited states from defunding certain abortion facilities. Trump also signed legislation repealing Obamacare's Independent Payment Advisory Board, which was also known as the death panels. Under Trump's Health and Human Services, they formed a new division protecting the rights of conscience and religious freedom. Trump gave more employers the opportunity to form association health plans, enabling more small businesses to join and affordably provide health insurance to their employees. And he expanded short-term health plans. President Trump created a precedent to drive down drug prices for patients, negotiating with multiple leading drug companies to halt or reverse price increases. And in 2017, the Food and Drug Administration set a record for generic drug approvals, saving consumers nearly 9 billion dollars. In 2018, he saved seniors an estimated 320 million dollars on prescription drugs by making changes to their Medicare program. He expanded health care options for terminally ill patients, by signing the Right-to-Try Legislation, and he signed legislation to improve the National Suicide Hotline. And in order to advance childhood cancer research and improve treatments, Trump signed the most comprehensive Childhood Cancer Legislation ever place into law.

In October 2017, Donald Trump declared the opioid crisis a nationwide public health emergency. He formed a commission to combat drug addiction and the opioid crisis, which founded several policies to tackle the ongoing opioid crisis. They created an initiative to stop opioid abuse and reduce the drug supply, introducing new measures to keep the dangerous drugs out of America's communities. In 2017 and 2018, they led two National Prescription Drug Take Back Days, both times collecting a record number of unneeded and expired prescription drugs. Battling the opioid addiction problem that has plagued our nation has been a priority to President Trump and his administration.

President Trump has done so much to improve veterans' affairs because their services were so inadequate. Under Trump's leadership, they created a White House VA Hotline to help veterans. They increased transparency and accountability at the VA by launching an online "access and quality tool," providing veterans with access to wait time and quality of care data. Trump signed the Veteran's Affairs Accountability Act, which expanded the tele-health services, walk-in-clinics, and same-day urgent primary and mental health care. And he signed additional legislation to modernize the claims and appeal process at the VA. Trump's administration enacted a complete reform to the VA system with the Veterans Affairs Mission Act. This act consolidated and strengthened VA community care programs. It provided extensive funding, which enabled the VA to modernize their infrastructure and equipment, strengthened the VA's ability to hire and retain quality healthcare professionals, and provided for the Veterans Choice Program. They also expanded the eligibility for the Family Caregivers Program. Trump has given veterans more efficient and quality care services.

America has become energy independent as a result of the Trump administration's industrious policies. President Trump ended the war on the coal industry. He revoked the anti-coal Clean Power Plan of Obama's administration, and he proposed the Affordable Clean Energy Rule as a replacement. Trump rolled back the Stream Protection Rule. And thus in 2017, coal exporting numbers are up over 60 percent. Trump also withdrew from the disastrous Paris Climate Agreement, which was projected to have led to 6.5 million fewer jobs in the United States by 2040, and the cost for America would be nearly 3 trillion dollars. Trump enacted a presidential memorandum to clear obstacles with the construction of the Dakota Access Pipeline and the Keystone XL Pipeline. Under the Trump administration, achieving its highest level in United States history, America is now the largest crude oil producer in the world. Our country has become a natural gas exporter for the first time in six decades. In August 2018, Trump offered areas to lease for offshore gas and oil in the Gulf of Mexico, and he negotiated an expansion of offshore drilling as part of his energy strategy. Trump also revoked the Hydraulic Fracturing Rule of Obama's administration, which was projected to cost nearly 32 million dollars annually.

Everyone said he could not do it, and the hyperbolic naysayers were proven wrong yet again! On June 13, 2018, President Donald J. Trump successfully met in Singapore for a historic summit with North Korean President Kim Jong-Un, which marked a pathway to denuclearization and peace on the Korean Peninsula. These leaders met in February 2019 in Hanoi, Vietnam, and again, on June 30, 2019, at the Korean Demilitarized Zone. Since then, they have worked through their own written communications, and meetings of their high-ranking national officials have also been held, making for unbelievable progress. Not only did North Korea halt their nuclear program and missile testing, they also negotiated the return of the remains of our American soldiers, who had been missing in action since the Korean War. While recent disturbing rumblings have stirred in North Korea, we can remain hopeful of the response of our president, who seems to handle these foreign policies very well.

Trump placed sanctions against seven Russian oligarchs and the companies they own or control, who profited from Russia's destabilizing activities, with their offensive cyber capabilities. And he released a strong and comprehensive United States' cyber strategy.

With Trump as commander-in-chief, ISIS has lost all its territory.

American hostages have been freed from captivity and brought home to the United States.

The Jewish people and Christians alike celebrated when President Trump moved the United States Embassy in Israel to Jerusalem. He was the first president to keep this promise! Amen!

Trump helped to win the United States' bid for the 2028 Summer Olympics to be in Los Angeles, California, and the US-Mexico-Canada's combined bid for 2026 World Cup.

These victories are just the tip of the iceberg, and there are so many more glorious accomplishments from the past three and a half years of the Trump administration. Our businessman president knows how to hire the most qualified and effective experts to successfully guide him as he runs our country. You can see that he listens intently to their advice, as he weighs the benefits and acts to best serve the nation and her citizens. "We the People" chose the right man for the job, as ruler of the free world!

For Thoughtful Consideration

Can you claim to be a tolerant, kind, and/or loving person in some circumstances and still be a hater in other circumstances? Can we hate something that someone has done or said and still love that person? Can we understand that the things that people say and do can be heard and seen differently based on the context in which they are presented? What if someone intentionally wanted you to hate someone based on their own personal agenda and they portrayed that person as despicable, would you be okay with that? I have a really hard time condoning that behavior. How about you?

CHAPTER 11

Silent Majority

"If you don't have anything nice to say, don't say anything at all."
—Known as Thumper's rule in Disney's film *Bambi*

A nasty comment here or an inappropriate gesture there, however if we protest, we get targeted as an intolerant monster. So if we silently let things slide, the nastiness increases and the inappropriateness becomes more severe. Those of us that condone these negative behaviors are known as the silent majority. We have been silently sitting back and watching the decline of our American values, morals, and principles. One of the reasons that we are in the mess that we are in today is because we have looked the other way too many times. It is our lack of courage that leads to our unwillingness in speak up. Therefore, in all fairness, we, the silent majority, should take ownership of being a large part of the problems that is currently dividing our country today.

The silent majority consist of mostly people who do not want to be badgered by the angry politically opinionated crazies who plague our society. We are the citizens who want to live in peace, not protest. We want to get along with our fellow countrymen. So we do not state our opinion. Some of us do not even want to talk about politics or social stances for fear of an argument erupting. We may be known as people pleasers, who simply wish to remain non-confrontational.

Or maybe we just do not care because we do not think we can make a difference anyway.

The silent group are the ones who have heard their ideology previously shot down by the loud obnoxious opposing people. And although they are smaller in size, this opposing group can be extremely intimidating. They are the noisy minority! Sometimes, they can be abusive, condescending, and even threatening. They may even lie to push a point that they cannot otherwise prove. In most cases, you find no chance for a reasonable debate, so you do not offer your opinion or even present facts.

You may fall into the category of not being silent, among like-minded people. When we are around those who think similarly to our thoughts, we love it because we can finally share our opinion without condemnation. Those likeminded individuals validate how we think and make us realize that we are not deplorable, after all. We can speak our minds freely to those comrades, and they may sympathize with how we feel.

Suppression of the Conservative Voice

> *Conservatives think Liberals are stupid.*
> *Liberals think Conservatives are evil.*
> —Charles Krauthammer

I am not sure just when the gloves came off for me. But it was at that time I realized I was not helping the political environment by remaining silent. In fact, I started to feel as though my being quiet was somehow my being complicit. Could I be unwittingly letting our country lose its finest qualities? Could my becoming aware of and then simply watching this divisive plot, which was unfolding, make me part of the problem? I knew it was time to stand up for what is right and just. I knew it was time to fight back for our country's sake. And most importantly, I knew I could not let my family, friends, and this nation's people continue to be manipulated by twisted liberal narratives. By seeking and speaking the truth, we can save those we care about from being deliberately blinded and angered with constant lies and deception. Our voices must be heard as compassionate, opening the eyes and ears of misled people, to prevent them from falling victim to these intentional forms of mind control and oppression.

For decades, conservative thinkers have not only been under attack by their political opponents, but also by Liberal professors in universities, celebrities in Hollywood, and journalists in the mainstream media. These assaults are often gross character fabrications accompanied by mocking and belittling. Leaving conservative thinkers unfairly portrayed and ultimately silenced. Because the Democrats and Progressives had made it so unpopular to be labeled a Conservative, those who harbored right-wing ideas often kept their opinions to themselves. Still today, left-wing bullies use intimidation to send right-wing voices into hiding. Please do not forget, under the Obama administration's abusive silencing tactics, Conservatives were being singled out and targeted. One example was the Internal Revenue Service scandal, which went after conservative groups, such as the Tea Party. These types of attacks are meant to quiet activism coming from Right-Wing groups. Now, after such apparent schemes, fewer Conservatives are bowing down in a submissive retreat mode. Many patriots are determined to stand up for their rights, as put forth in our First Amendment for the freedom of speech and expression.

As a reminder, a strong disadvantage for Conservatives is that they are represented by only seven news outlets, compared to the Liberal's thirty-two outlets, which limits their ability to reach as many people in the general public. Conservative's news outlets tend to honestly present facts within their commentary, which becomes an issue for them, when their factual message is disputed with lies. Liberal's news outlets often co-mingle propaganda with accusations and use speculation to twist the truth into what they conveniently call their truth. Then if these Liberal commentators need to retract some fictitious story, only a small part of their original audience may hear the retraction. This causes most of the confusing mixed messages that have plagued and divided our nation. Then running the risk of misinterpretation, the mixed messages make it difficult for the conservative debater to accurately present their position on issues because those issues have been contradicted with a lie. Disputing a lie is never easy and leaves the speaker of the truth defensive and frustrated.

Conservative speakers tend to be less confrontational or aggressive unless pushed to their limits. We spend a great deal of our time fighting for our good name and defending the derogatory messages that have been planted against us. When the Liberals portray Conservatives as evil, this deception makes our country and her people weak, and in the end, it only benefits those greedy, rich, and power-mongering elites who wish to divide us. Remember President Trump's words, "When America is united, America is totally unstoppable."

You cannot place the blame on all Radicals. Most are unwitting accomplices because the fundamental premise of their radicalism stems from an injustice being perpetrated against them. Many Radicals have been completely fooled by Liberals that they admire and trust. It is only natural that those Radicals, who have been strongly influenced by those flagrant liars and conniving provocateurs, would see Conservatives as hateful and the enemy. These are forms of manipulation that are overlooked by many Radicals and other Liberals too. The tactic of using emotional persuasion to paint the Conservative in a negative light. This strategy, used mostly by the Liberal media, involves creating untrue heartbreaking stories which reflect badly on innocent Conservatives, thus leaving the unsuspecting Radicals and Liberals feeling justified in their ensuing anger and provoked intimidation. This can leave most Conservatives unwilling to take a stand on any political issues because their opinion has been attached to demonizing characteristics. Shutting down all possibility of a rational debate because defending oneself becomes futile and frustrating. Rendering the Conservative silent becomes an ongoing destructive pattern every election cycle. All Americans, with both right- and left-leaning ideologies, lose the truthful objectivity to make critical decisions regarding issues when voting, which determines the important matters of their fate and well-being.

The most damaging outcome of the political adversaries is the constant loose labeling of each other with vicious names. Labeling an opponent with ugly "isms" and phobias is the #1 cause of most of the divisions among the diverse groups of people in our nation. This perpetuates hurtful feelings based on some of the personal qualities that identify us, such as our race, gender, sexual orientation, religion, and creed. Liberal politicians have used the strategy of labeling their conservative opponents to alienate them from large groups of diverse people. While vying for the public's votes, these Liberal politicians create the division that we are suffering from across our nation. These thuglike attacks are cruel and divisive, yet they do not care, so long as they can secure your vote. Conservatives become crushed every election cycle when Liberals demonize the character of their opponent with false accusations that leave them defenseless and sometimes speechless. This affects both the conservative candidate and the voter.

Now, I am not saying that the Liberal politicians are not attacked by their Conservative opponents, both Democrats and Republicans are guilty of malicious rhetoric designed to damage their adversaries in the hopes of getting your vote. Frankly, it is the lies that have perpetuated anger and hate, and those lies laid a foundation for the destructive birthing of an era of political correctness.

The PC Police

Political correctness became a term used to describe language or policies that are intended to avoid offending a group of people. Determining what is socially acceptable dialogue became up for debate, and these debates sometimes caused the triggering of more and deeper hurt feelings. Using inclusive phrases to refrain from any insensitivity could sometimes appear equally awkward. Speech grew strained through the prism of constant scrutiny and due to the inflicted guilt associated with it. However, the gravest point of the problems with political correctness emerged through a group known as the PC police.

Although the name PC police implies some regard for law and order, it stirs an injustice within its purpose. Firstly, it tends to isolate groups even further from each other. These marginalized people feel more grieved and defensive because of the hyperbolic reaction of the PC police rather than the sting of the misguided comment. Though a flip statement may cause pain, we all understand how easily things can be misinterpreted, and intentions are rarely malicious.

While the Left-Wing Liberals designate the terms associated with political correctness, they use it to accuse the Right-Wing Conservatives of being horrible haters. Based on an unwittingly incorrect use of words, they determine what is hate speech and what is not. This attack on the Conservative voices is intended to send them into a role of passive submission. The result is an ensuing drama because in response, the Right often accuse these Liberal PC police of being an enemy of the people. Provoking this farce and festering anger ultimately causes the ongoing pain and division amongst our citizens. Therefore, it is the PC police that set the tone and pace of our civil discourse. Their demands for monitored speech conforming with their ideology leads to a mob mentality, which flames the fires of chaos in our society. And as far as they are concerned, "We the People" surrendering to them, the mob, is our only option.

Another issue that may become a dire situation is by not calling out an observation based on the desire to be politically correct, you could have a detrimental outcome. This may hinder the ability to tackle issues of social importance. Being cautious in how we approach the problems that face our nation can significantly alter our power to be effective. Political correctness should not overrule criminal activity because then, our country runs the risk of everyone involved becoming victims in a pending crisis when people's safety and security are in danger. For example, the heated debate over fixing the challenges at our southern border. The safety of our citizens depends on our capability of securing our border from potential criminals. That fact does not need to become a racial issue. However, it is used as a weapon by Left-Wing candidates to label their Right-Wing adversaries. Everyone knows that there are both criminals and refugees attempting to illegally cross our borders at undesignated areas. Those immigrants who wish to enter our country properly can do so at designated ports of entry. Taking emotional warfare out of any scenario and stating only the facts of a matter is crucial. The truth is that when immigration is not done by the rule of law, both the American citizens and the illegal immigrants run the risk of a dangerous and potential deadly outcome. Whatever the result, any fault can strictly be placed at the hands of those who lack regard for safety, security, and the rule of law. And the benefits of a safe and secure border are shared mutually by both countries and their citizens.

President Trump has tried to calm the public discourse, by ending the viciousness of the PC police, who use political correctness to provoke anger by lying about intentionality and motives. Trump's requests for unity have been shunned by the Left. And the PC police's constant use of attack by misquoting and taking his statements out of context has been reckless and cruel, only making unity impossible. Using the race card to bludgeon one's opponents is a stale and overused tactic. Every day Americans are seeing through the labeling strategies of those Left-Wing politicians, who simply have run out of ideas and have no accomplishments to excite their voter base. Their campaigns mean more to them than the people whom they are elected to serve.

These PC police are just another group silencing anyone who does not agree with their liberal ideology. Their use of identity politics, driven with baseless accusations, has sown a gross amount of pain and division throughout our nation, with their one goal of gaining popularity with voters. By using identity politics and political correctness together, these Left-Wing politicians and their allies in the Liberal elite crowd have persuasively misled large groups of people, including those who are not paying attention to succumb to the abuse of emotional blackmail. Therefore, rather than conforming to the mob of angry dictators, with the fear of being misjudged, the Conservative remains submissively silent.

Under President Trump, we are finally catching on to the scare tactics and verbal attacks of the PC police. His brave action to neutralize their effectiveness has exposed their playbook, so they can no longer manipulate us. Their oppressive rants are no longer convincing. Now, Conservatives are feeling emboldened to fight back, seek their justice, and speak their truth.

Censorship

Google has become a very disturbing tech giant, and if you are not afraid of them, you should be. Google dominates 70 percent of online advertising, and they control the news outlets that have access to those advertisers, based on the content of the material that they deem suitable. This very forceful liberal entity can ban the Far-Right journalism that they do not agree with, by labeling it hate speech. And currently, Google has unchecked power where and when information is released because they have special immunities from the United States Congress.

When Left-Wing tech giants twist the truth to suit their political narrative, our perception of reality is at stake. If they are willing to distort reality, then they can sway our thoughts to suit their agenda. When our thoughts do not conform with theirs, Google, YouTube, Twitter, and Facebook have the power to strong arm and stifle our rights to free speech and our ability to convey our messages. It is intentional and their strategy is to silence those who stand in their way.

I have been very wary of Google, YouTube, Twitter, and Facebook since prior to the 2016 presidential election. It became increasing clear that the use of partiality in their search engines, and the shadow banning techniques of these social media companies was very eschewed in their integrity. You would think that they would have no biases; however, it became apparently clear that they presented favorable information about one candidate and unfavorable about the other. Also, there was no honest fact checking being done by these determiners of what we should hear and what we should see. And the fact checker Snopes was found to be inaccurate and left leaning too.

These self-proclaimed pillars of virtue, who profess to always take the moral high ground, were intentionally using domestic interference to manipulate the voters and outcome of our elections.

For Thoughtful Consideration

When we are silent during an injustice, are we condoning negative behaviors? If we are silent, do we allow our likeminded friends to be bullied? Does our silence make us complicit?

CHAPTER 12

Politics and Religion

If my people who are called by my name humble themselves, and pray and seek my face and turn from their wicked ways, then I will hear from heaven and will forgive their sin and heal their land.
—2 Chronicles 7:14

I s America a nation based on faith? Although the United Sates Constitution does not specifically designate any particular religion, it mentions freedom of religion and the right to assemble, as in churches. The Founding Fathers and their families were of Christian-based beliefs. You could see this in their first writings of pamphlets, articles, and books. Throughout the course of our history, God was an influential part of our American system of government. In his farewell address to the nation on September 17, 1796, George Washington forewarned, "Of all the dispositions and habits which lead to political prosperity, religion and morality are indispensable supports…reason and experience both forbid us to expect that national morality can prevail in exclusion of religious principle. It is substantially true that virtue or morality is a necessary spring of popular government."

It is faith that has inspired America toward the growth and renewal in her most critical and defining moments. During the civil war, Lincoln drew on the strength of his Christianity and God with prayerful words to and for the nation. World War II was thought of by Franklin D. Roosevelt and Dwight Eisenhower as a fight to keep the Christian principles of human rights and freedoms from being taken over by those who wanted a tyrannical rule. The New Deal Welfare Program was one that was influenced by faith. At the heart of the rivalry between Russia and America, John F. Kennedy and Ronald Reagan, both referred to the cold war, which lasted several decades, were the struggles between the godlessness of atheist Communism and the Judeo-Christian freedoms. Christian principles also motivated the Civil Rights Movement, between 1954 and 1968. As Reverend Martin Luther King Jr. wrote in his letter from a Birmingham jail, "One day the South will know that when these disinherited children of God sat down at lunch counters, they were in reality standing up for what is best in the American Dream and for the most sacred values in our Judeo-Christian heritage, thereby bringing our nation back to those great wells of democracy which were dug deep by the founding fathers in their formulation of the Constitution and the Declaration of Independence."

In 2012, the Democrat National Committee removed God and Israel from their platform. They denied that America is a nation which was built on a love for God and the traditions of Christianity. Their dismissal of Israel, as our spiritual and ideological partner, pointed us toward a battle to destroy the Western cultures. Most obvious to those who were paying attention, the Democrat Party's desire was to push America away from their strength in God and to enslave her people to a reliance on a powerful government. The Leftist hostility to Christian grew more intense as we watch our beloved faith-based holidays being redefined. Their rejection of God was blatant, as they mocked and booed Him during their 2012 DNC Convention. Who's crying now?

You have been told by lofty politicians, self-serving religious zealots, and weak Christians that religion and politics do not mix. For those dishonest politicians, it works in their favor for you to keep God out of governmental issues because they know that God would not condone their devious ways. As for the religious zealots, there may be a few reasons for clinging to the separation of church and state issue, and those most likely have to do with controversial content and its inability to draw larger memberships and more money. However, the separation of church and state does not mean no faith. Our Founders met regularly in the public square to have religious ceremonies. These Founding Fathers did not hide their faith and considered their Christian principles crucial to the well-being of the country.

For Christians and other religious people who would rather not stand by their God's laws, they may believe that God can somehow be ignored by using the government as an excuse because Godly principles are not always convenient for them to uphold. Have religious leaders of the Christian faith been losing track of the requests God makes for His children to evangelize to all the nations? By advancing the Kingdom of God, we honor our God and His desire for nations to be His. As Jesus requests of His followers in Matthew 28:19–20, "Therefore go and make disciples of all nations, baptizing them in the name of the Father and of the Son and of the Holy Spirit, and teaching them to obey everything I have commanded you. And surely, I am with you always, to the very end of the age."

One simple concept that we see repeated often in the Bible is the lesson that our Heavenly Father and our Lord Jesus teach us: if God's people obeyed His rules, He blessed them abundantly, and if God's people turned away from Him, He leaves them on their own, and consequently, things do not go well for those people or their land. Repentance, prayer, and obedience lead to blessings and joy. When the land is filled with the power and peace of His Holy Spirit, the territories flourish. With thoughtful examination, even the unbeliever can be aware of the wonder of God when they observe His presence or lack of presence in situations across our nation. Let us honestly think about how our God works and how He reveals Himself in America and throughout the world.

America was losing her moral compass by gradually taking God away from her citizens. The political agendas were being pushed further and further away from God's principles and standards. Schools were no longer praying together, and yet we wonder why our children lack proper educations or why there is violence on campuses.

God's name has been removed from government and federal buildings, public institutions, and our currency, and yet we wonder why our finances and economy have suffered. You want to strip Him and His values from the nation, yet you wonder where He is during your darkest moments.

America, the devil has been trespassing, and he refuses to leave! You are letting him have free reign, and he is wreaking division and terror. Am I exaggerating? You be my judge, but do not turn a blind eye. Homelessness, drug overdoses, suicides, violent crimes, child abuse, pedophilia, sexual perversion, human trafficking, fear, rage, disease, oppression, and desperation are the dark world of Satan's Kingdom. He laughs with arrogance at this modern-day America, he revels in her destruction and despair! However, Satan loathes the America of our beloved Founding Fathers, a land of unity, justice, and dreams.

Our sinful nature has been passed off as acceptable, so do we have the right to expect our God to save us? You can witness Hollywood pushing the envelope further and further toward more vulgarity and violence. The perversion and brutality in films and television have become intensely obscene and vicious. Audiences with any innocence or sensitivity are left feeling truly uncomfortable. Do you question why our children are so confused about the difference between right and wrong? Nudity in art and entertainment can also bear a dangerous effect when determining for a society what is beautiful. We see actors and models, who are touched up with perfect makeup and hairstyles, with their Photoshopped bodies telling us what looks good and what does not. Holding us all to a high standard, that is sometimes not attainable. Forming our thoughts and our children's opinions about body image by Hollywood's standards can be unhealthy. It affects the way that we feel about ourselves and one another. Your pornography and graphic sexual situations are not fit for a society that wants uphold any standards of strong morals and ethical values. Christians, religious, and spiritual people of all faiths recognize that the lack of integrity in our entertainment industry is promoting mental instability within our nation, taking everything that is good from a world that needs good.

Is it any wonder why our country is riddled with drug addiction, brutal rapes, and horrible crimes? Video games have become so extremely violent that our youth are becoming lost in virtual realities, which leads them to become unable to cope with their own realities. Is it any wonder that they pick up weapons to harm others or commit suicides? By romanticizing the use of weapons with bloodcurdling violence, Hollywood, you did this to our youth. Devastation is the result, and it goes on and on. Americans know the endless tragic stories and heartfelt grief. All the while, movie stars, famous athletes, and musicians, who are nothing but a bunch of whining narcissists preening themselves in front of their adoring fans with self-righteous indignation, spew political barbs to push liberal elitist agendas. And yet who do those shallow self-absorb morons blame? You cannot blame God! You did not want him around! You banished Him! You cannot blame the drugs or the weapons, they are inanimate objectives!

Human beings and our sinful natures are what inspire the actions of our people. Our children learn by our examples, and it is our responsibility to monitor what we let them be exposed to in their fragile world. Basic principles of goodness and kindness are what bring happiness, genuine love, and peaceful coexistence to our homes and to our land. The Christian lifestyle offers those beautiful things as our Father promises in His word, and when we apply His word to our lives, we see blessed results. God says in Isaiah 41:10, "Do not fear: I am with you; do not be anxious: I am your God. I will strengthen you, I will help you, I will uphold you with My victorious right hand."

God gives you free will and many choices, but you must be prepared for the consequences of your actions. Understanding God is not difficult, He makes it easy. He wants to be a part of your life. All of it! You are either with Him or not. No gray areas. He does not want lukewarm, passive Christians. No compromising! Choose wisely! I realize, when you have Satan on your left shoulder telling you life will be more exciting with him, it can be very tempting because he is the master manipulator and the great deceiver. However, trust our faithful Lord, who is on your right shoulder, when he warns you, per-

version and lies will lead to destruction and despair. With your obedience and trust, you open yourself up to a relationship with our one
true and living God who loves us deeply. My strong Christian views
are in alignment with what the Bible tells all of us and what I have
come to learn on my lifelong journey with my Heavenly Father. I
realize that most religious people are victims of different experiences
on their walk with God. And by sharing these views (and frankly,
the views of this entire book), I speak from my path's perspective,
which may only represent half of the population or even less. Some
Christians, and even some pastors, rather pray quietly and not voice
their opinions, possibly due to that risk of pushing half the world
away. And I truly understand that might be why it becomes convenient for them to say, "I do not mix politics with religion."

Courage to awaken those in need can be a gift that the Holy
Spirit fills you with and guide you through. Remember, it is not
loving and kind to be complacent while you watch your cities burn
and your neighbors suffer loss. We need our Christian leaders to take
roles in their communities, stepping outside their comfort zones
behind the walls of their church buildings. Boldly making an impact
on the decisions that affect their congregants and even the lost sheep
in their areas. These are the times that people need the words of hope
from evangelists who have an opportunity to give the truth of God's
encouraging word. And we as Christians must also take our place in
reaching out in our local towns, to be good role models sharing God's
Good News. There are Christians uniting across this great nation
because they realize America is doomed without God. We know that
our Lord Jesus says in His Sermon on the Mount, Matthew 5:13–16,
that we are to be the salt of the earth and light of the world, influencing others for good and guiding them from darkness. Political issues
are faith issues, and we need our religious leaders to speak with strong
guidance regarding governmental policies that effect our well-being
as God's people.

Some religious leaders have been silenced by the Johnson
Amendment from speaking out against political issues that do not
adhere to biblical standards. These churches that are under this
Section 501(c)(3) for tax exemptions must refrain from endorsing or

opposing political candidates. On May 4, 2017, President Donald Trump signed an Executive Order "to defend the freedom of religion and speech" for the purpose of easing the Johnson Amendment's restrictions. Because political issues affect the lives of Christians throughout our country, lifting these restrictions are beneficial, giving pastors and religious leaders an open platform to educate their congregations on the ramifications of some of the governmental policies and stances of our times, and alerting members of the politicians promote those agendas. Voting for politicians and propositions that support faith-based policies, according to what God's word requires of us, gives us the opportunity to support our nation as a Godly people should. Making us worthy as a country who wish to receive God's blessings. It may sound foreign to some, but to most believers, I would hope that it sounds *obvious*!

One more point, regarding the importance of placing good moral and righteous principles at the foundation of our nation, and this goes for faithful Jews, Mormons, Jehovah's Witnesses, Muslims, and other peace-loving religious groups, as well as Christians, we know that evil exists. Evil is what is at the root of the divisions that cause Americans suffering and chaos. Satan is at work, causing a great disunity, rage, and anger with his lies and deception. This devil has taken over our country: in our schools, in our homes, in media, in arts, in entertainment, and so much more. His tricks and schemes confuse those who are weak in their religious beliefs and especially targets those who are unbelievers. America has fallen victim to this evil because citizens have let Satan invade while pushing our value systems out. When we recognize this evil one and become aware of his tactics, we will win our country back from his wicked grip. Prayer and unity must be our strategy to fight back!

Racism

God created man in His own image, male and female He created them.
—Genesis 1:27

There is no place for racism in a Christian heart! Period! Let me clearly and bluntly state it, you cannot call yourself a Christian and be a racist. We are all God's children, and He has created us beautifully in His image. It is the awesomeness of our God, who loves all His children, that He would make us each special and unique within His family. We have different looks, sounds, talents, and characteristics that also give us our purpose here on earth. And furthermore, whether someone is Christian or another faith or not religious at all, a Christian has a respect for *all* peoples, because as our Savior commands us, "Love one another, as I have loved you."

Unfortunately, America has a deep history of racism, which we have worked so hard to atone for and get past. It is her citizens, who have been horribly racist, that have perpetuated the obstacles that cripple our ability to heal and move forward. America is *not* a racist nation! It is the opposite. Our country is founded to be a melting pot of diversity. If America were racist, we would not be welcoming immigrants and refugees to our country. We welcome those our love our land and wish to be a part of her American Way. Our Declaration of Independence, written by Thomas Jefferson, states, "We hold these truths to be self-evident, that all men are created equal, that they are endowed by their Creator with certain unalienable Rights, that among these are Life, Liberty and the pursuit of Happiness." The mantra of our founding document is clear that the United States of America is a nation of their Creator for the equality of all its citizenry. Our country is based on unity; however, there are evil men in our land who are racists and they do despicable acts. We must not conflate the differences between who we are as a nation and those wicked ones who do not represent us.

After reading through many of our Founding Fathers documents, I find no evidence that slavery was thought of in a positive way. It is a stain of shame on the fabric of our past.

In April 1786, George Washington spoke out against slavery in his Letter to Morris, when he wrote, "There is not a man living who wishes more sincerely than I do, to see a plan adopted for the abolition of it [slavery]."

In 1789, Ben Franklin said in An Address to the Public from the Pennsylvania Society for Promoting the Abolition of Slavery, "Slavery is…an atrocious debasement of human nature."

The second president, John Adams, was not a slave owner. In June 1819, in his Letter to Evans, he wrote, "Every measure of prudence, therefore, ought to be assumed for the eventual total extirpation of slavery from the United States…I have, through my whole life, held the practice of slavery in…abhorrence."

The Conservative Union Officers, who fought, bled, and died for the abolition of slavery, did so with a heart of compassion and reconciliation to heal the nation.

During his Peoria Speech in October 1854, Abraham Lincoln stated, "The plain unmistakable spirit of that age [the founding era], towards slavery, was hostility to the principle, and toleration, only by necessity."

In the words of Dr. Ben Carson, he says that under the leadership of President Trump, "We the people will recognize, despite all the forces to the contrary, that we are not each other's enemies."

There are also race-baiting traitors among our citizens, who hate our country, and it is their goal that they get us to hate America as well. They want to fundamentally change and destroy our strong nation. These provocateurs of racial disunity want Americans to remain divided, weak, and at each other's throats. While we want to be united patriots, with the common desires of building our nation's economy and keeping our people safe, their treasonous intent is to ruin everything that we hold dear. They twist the truth, stoke our anger, and misrepresent our intentions. And when there is not enough visible rioting, looting, and crime to be seen by the onlooking public, they create more by paying for rowdy and violent activists to show up and give their destructive illusion. Why? Power!

Recently, we all have witnessed unspeakable and horrible acts of racism. I do not know one person who was not united in the agreement that these racist acts were purely evil and deserve the maximum punishment for the perpetrators. We are mourning and suffering as a nation, yet some celebrities and elitists are using our grief to condemn those who they oppose politically. We are afraid to express our sadness because anything we might say or do may be challenged as insensitive, not adequate, or even worse. Tenderness and genuine kindness are what our fellow Americans need, and yet aggressive agitators are what they are getting. Hate does not end hate, only love can heal the wounds of hatred. Our God is *love*!

Where are our spiritual leaders? Our hero Martin Luther King Jr. is the man that we need in these moments and his words should be filling our land. His niece, Alveda King, has been a calming voice of reason; she refers to Acts 17:26 when stating her view, "Of one blood God made all people to live together on the face of the earth."

She repeats her uncle Martin Luther King Jr.'s words, "We must learn to live together as brothers and sisters or perish together as fools."

She reminds us of what our President Donald J. Trump has often said, "We all bleed the same."

We have been so close to living happily ever after as one people, brothers and sisters, Americans. However, we fall backward into the same old traps because of some bad actors and evil doers. Those haters who know what they are doing in a systematic way, and those selfish haters who just do not care about anyone or anything. Some call themselves White Supremacists, although they are in no way superior to anyone. They are disgusting and must be lacking parental discipline. I would guess that they must be very insecure bullies, or they might have had some deeply negative childhood experiences. The other groups that revel in racism are these Left-Wing Elitists, Progressives, Socialists, and Marxists who are the agitators who promote violent activism. These monsters terrorize Americans by stirring up racism because they do not care about us as citizens, they simply thrive for power. And again, for them it is *all* about your beloved *vote*!

Those agitators are the worst, they destroy the black communities, as they have over the last sixty years, while claiming to be our friends. Dividing Americans is crucial to their plans. You have witnessed their destruction of good people's towns, small businesses, and places of employment, when they hire thugs to come along to incite rioting, looting, and violence. Leaving poor black families further in debt and more brokenhearted than ever. From a political standpoint, teaching our children to recognize these deceivers and warning them to stay away is one of the best gifts we can give them. And from a morals and values standpoint, we as parents giving our children hope and trust in a God who loves us, by taking them to good churches with strong spiritual leaders, is another great gift we can offer to our entire family. It has been proven that a family that prays together stays together! And it is also proven that the destruction of the traditional family unit is the root of the problems within poor communities. I mean this sincerely; the well-being of our youth, of all races, will hinder on the guidance of parental figures in their lives, and they will benefit from those who teach them a deep love and respect for themselves and others. If we keep God's word as an instruction manual for educating our children, and for our own wisdom and knowledge throughout life, we cannot go wrong. Offering hope to those who suffer at the hands of racial inequality, and with the help of God's love, we can heal the wounds of racism. Stand strong in the reality that America is a country which has been built firmly as a melting pot of diversity, fighting against prejudice and segregation with perpetual strides toward a patriotic unity.

Sexual Bigotry

Another form of hate is sexual bigotry. Again, there is no place for any kind of bigotry in a Christian's heart. However, keeping one's private life private would be my preference. Sometimes, our government becomes involved in social issues that should be left alone.

A favorite restaurant in our area made its political statement when their restrooms became gender neutral. The first two occasions that I used the area, it just proved to feel awkward, but the third time was horrible. As I was exiting the stall, I could see three little girls at the sink area washing their hands, and the littlest girl was visibly shaken and upset. I asked the two older girls, who appeared to be about eight years old, if they needed any help. One of them said her little sister had opened the door to a man with his pants down revealing his naked body, and although she still needed to go potty, she was petrified to open another stall door. I showed her to the stall that I had just come out of and waited for her to exit. I imagine this little girl will be very bothered by this incident for what might be years. Those scary and vivid images do not leave your mind when you are that young, as they probably would not for an adult either.

I do not speak for all Christians because many of us have been raised in varying religious denominations with different priests and pastors, so our circumstances may not be alike. However, religious people who practice their faith know that God's word is our guide, and we must examine and live it as we determine what is acceptable and unacceptable to Him. Each of us is responsible for the choices we make and how we choose to live is very personal. Being self-righteous is also unacceptable to God, so as a Christian, we walk a fine line between being righteous and being self-righteous. While we know that we are not to judge others, we know that we must recognize sin. And yet we are to leave judgment up to God and simply love in all things.

Levels of tolerance and acceptance can mean different things to different Christians and religious people, but most of us agree that although it is not our place to judge others, we are also not to condone wrongdoing. If it sounds like I am defending our stances as Christians, it is because our feelings and what God's word says can be quite different things. And depending on your spiritual walk throughout your life and which belief system you adhere to, your ideas about what is right and what is wrong may differ. But faithful Christians know that hate is not associated with our role as God's children. However, a couple things we can all agree on are that, what are the gray areas for us are not gray areas for God and the subject of sexual orientation and what is acceptable has become hypersensitive and very touchy in an ever-evolving world.

Our God gives us a Holy Bible and He tells us that it is His word. It is the instruction manual that we follow to learn about the works of God and how He works. In reading His word, we learn how to recognize Him guiding us through our lives and we see His hand on our nation. The Holy Bible is the textbook we use and abide by in our walk with Him. Most Christians follow the rule of "love the sinner but hate the sin." Which can be quite easy most of the time because we know that we too are sinners. Have human beings decided to be the determiners of what sin is though? Or have they decided to simply sin regardless because their God will forgive them? Has God's commands made the sinner turn their back on God entirely because they would rather be free to sin than follow some of His boring laws? Does watching others live a worldly life make sin seem more normalized? Maybe God's word has changed? Or maybe God has changed His mind? No, that cannot be it! We know that our God is clear and faithful to His word. Maybe we have misinterpreted His word? That might be more realistic. There is a lot to think about on this one, but one thing will never change: as Christians, we must love.

Christians regard traditional marriage and family values, as they align with God's word. However, our government gets its nose into places that put our citizens at odds with each other. Could it be their ultimate plan to keep us divided and weak? As society keeps moving its boundaries further away from God's word, Christians are thrust in the middle of reactionary political issues, making Christians the targets of endless persecution.

In this era of gay marriage, respecting one's life choices should go both ways. So as a gay person wishes to be treated with dignity, they too must be respectful of the freedoms of others. Christian business owners have been persecuted for keeping true to God's word. The Liberal Left has not honored those proprietor's constitutional rights to refuse to perform services according to their religious beliefs. I stand by my fellow Christian's freedom to withhold services to anyone when a request is contrary to their godly principles. Business owners, as well as other citizens, should be permitted to practice their faith as they see fit. Patrons should always be respectful and simply choose another place of business who can offer them the services they desire.

Pro-Life

God gives you free will and many choices. God does not make mistakes. He is the giver of life and every life is precious to Him and those lives should also be precious to the Christian.

From the moment of conception, a human being starts life in their mother's womb. There is no disputing that we all began our lives and our bodies were forming from that single moment. This is a scientific fact. All of us are given the potential for our futures at that fateful time. We are all human beings worthy of the lives we have been given. The mother and her baby are two bodies. Yes! The mother has the responsibility to care for her own body while she nurtures her child's. Responsibility is the key. Taking responsibility for one's actions and the consequences of those actions is not just a Christian issue, but also an honorable way to live.

I stand firm in the woman's right to choose to have sex, I stand by her right to choose to use birth control, and I stand by her right to choose to give her baby up for adoption. And I will always stand by her child's right to life. Protecting the sanctity of innocent life from conception to natural death is not just the position of the Christian, but it is the position of God.

"Women's health" has become a deceptive front for Planned Parenthood in their rouse to make abortion acceptable. No pro-life Christian should be forced to pay the taxes funding Planned Parenthood on any level, while they are performing abortions. Every side of the political aisle will agree that we all support women's health issues, so condemning pro-life Christians as anti-women is a grotesque lie. If Planned Parenthood ended all abortion procedures, both Liberal and Conservative Americans would support them as a family health care facility.

Roe v. Wade has become a severely contentious debate which has divided the conscience of the nation. And I fear that it will continually haunt America with unending battles and strife. Watching the appointment of Justice Brett Kavanaugh to the Supreme Court was mixed with highly diverse emotions sweeping the entire country. It became obvious to reasonable citizens that the Radical Left and the Democratic Party, with their never-ending "resistance," railroaded the process to fight his approval. To let a respected man and his lovely family be attacked in such a heartless way proved, to me and many others, evil attacking good has been a strong driving force throughout our political environment, mainstream media, and Hollywood. The power-mongering Democrat Politicians and their Radical Liberal base can deliver all the moral preening and virtue signaling they can muster, but we realize that it is merely egotistical babel with a motive. Anyone who could choose to do such despicable acts to garner votes has lost all sense of integrity. And in the end, God wins!

*****

I am not a biblical scholar nor an authority on any topic, I am simply sharing my feelings based on my life experiences. I am not holier than thou, I am a true work in progress. When it comes to the political and social stances that face our nation today, I think it is important to know my perspective as the writer because it can help you, the reader, to understand where the viewpoint originates. Ultimately, the goal of this material is for you to form your own organic thoughts without the possibility of my taint or bias. Religious people of many denominations may take different positions surrounding the political and social stances that affect our world, forming their own opinions depending on their level of spiritual awareness and commitment to their faith's beliefs. However, keep in mind that God's word is true and firm! I rather doubt that He has changed His mind over the centuries. He is not wishy-washy like us humans. He wants no compromises: we choose to have a relationship with Him or we do not. You decide! Are you all in?

Being mindful of God's will in the choices that we make, opens us up to receive His blessings and the peace of His Holy Spirit. And it is crucial that we stand firm in our convictions, even when making decisions at the ballot box, because what we condone and who we condone matters to God. The quality of our relationship with God depends on our commitment to Him, and when we vote, the outcome can either hinder or advance our ability to worship Him properly and freely.

It is impossible to keep all of God's commands. Jesus loves unconditionally, and He tells us to love as He does. Yes, we are all human, but when we are His, greater things are expected of us. On our best day, we are *all* sinners, so humbly we kneel before our God and ask for His forgiveness. Here are some important points, *when we repent,* God forgives us. Then after having been forgiven, we also know that in the Holy Bible, the book of John 8:11, Jesus says, "You are forgiven, go, and sin no more."

I have *not* yet found a verse that says, "You are forgiven so, go out and sin some more."

Condoning sinful behavior is wrong, too. Proverbs 24:25 says, "But to those who rebuke the wicked will be delight, and a good blessing will come upon them."

Rebuking can be as simply as not accepting negative behaviors. Cherishing strong ethics, sound morals and virtuous deeds in our homes, schools, and communities can advance peace and harmony. Promoting and rewarding what is good and condemning and punishing wrongdoing will bring about the love and healing that we desire in all aspects of the divisions in our nation. Have our parenting skills softened over the decades? Discipline gives our children inner strength and helps them see the value of a good work ethic. Teaching our children about the promises of their Heavenly Father is a way to offer them a sense of security and self-worth. Some of our Founding Fathers spoke regularly about Christian principles as a guideline to support our children's future. It was Dr. Benjamin Rush, one of the fifty-six signers of the Declaration of Independence, who said, "Let the children be carefully instructed in the principles and obligations of the Christian religion. This is the most essential part of education."

Occasionally, we may slip up and make mistakes, some of them very grave ones, but our intention as Christians, as in most religious groups, is to aspire to be the best person to the best of our ability. Leading by example is what we need our religious men and women to do, as our country has been crying out for direction. Their inspiring voices should be the guiding forces for our youth and in our communities, not just from the pulpit, but alongside the public during an ever-evolving swaying of the social environment in our nation. When stressful times and chaotic challenges are mounting those spiritual leaders should be out in front because they have a duty to offer people hope and calm with encouraging words while bringing them together in prayer.

POLITICS AND RELIGION

Some church leaders are emerging from the shadows, being a voice for the people of God and giving the Good News to the lost people of our nation. As a Roman Catholic, I was very proud of Archbishop Carlo Vigano, who on June 7, 2020 wrote a very brave and bold letter to President Trump. I highly recommend that you read his letter in its entirety (you can Google it). His thoughts aligned with my observations regarding this current "invisible enemy of all humanity" which is wreaking havoc throughout the world. In his words, the archbishop brings an awareness to President Trump:

> There are faithful Shepherds who care for the flock of Christ, but there are also mercenary infidels who seek to scatter the flock and hand the sheep over to be devoured by ravenous wolves. It is not surprising that these mercenaries are allies of the children of darkness and hate the children of light: just as there is a deep state, there is also a deep church that betrays its duties and forswears its proper commitments before God. Thus, the Invisible Enemy, whom good rulers fight against in public affairs, is also fought against by good shepherds in the ecclesiastical sphere.

He goes on by expressing his approval of the president:

> For the first time, the United States has in you a President who courageously defends the right to life, who is not ashamed to denounce the persecution of Christians throughout the world, who speaks of Jesus Christ and the right of citizens to freedom of worship. Your participation in the March for Life, and more recently your proclamation of the month of April as National Child Abuse Prevention Month, are actions that confirm which side you wish to fight on. And I

dare believe that both of us are on the same side
in this battle, albeit with different weapons.

And I love how the archbishop sums up the truth of our modern-day battle between good and evil in his statement:

> And it is disconcerting that there are
> Bishops—such as those whom I recently
> denounced—who, by their words, prove that
> they are aligned on the opposing side. They are
> subservient to the deep state, to globalism, to
> aligned thought, to the New World Order which
> they invoke ever more frequently in the name
> of a universal brotherhood which has nothing
> Christian about it, but which evokes the Masonic
> ideals of those who want to dominate the world
> by driving God out of the courts, out of the
> schools, out of families, and perhaps even out of
> churches."

It is always so refreshing for me to see religious men and women,
who recognize God's hand on our beloved president and see God's
will which is being done throughout America and around the globe.
We already know the end of this story of good versus evil. In the end,
God wins! And in the end, *we* win!

Our Praying President

We are shown the respect that our president has for our God and
God's children in this thoughtful quote by Donald Trump, "When
you open your heart to Patriotism, there is no room for prejudice.
The Bible tells us, 'How good and pleasant it is when God's people
live together in unity.'"

While our nation is so divided, I have witnessed President
Trump's endless requests for unity. I believe that Trump truly expected
that if he won the election of 2016, he would have been able to bring

our divided nation together. I realize the election process was highly contentious, and lots of mud had been slung on both sides; however, Trump placed uniting the people at the top of his agenda. His acceptance speech, in the middle of that fated night, was welcoming of all parties to embrace what he planned in "Making America Great Again" for every citizen. America being as she was always intended, united as "One Nation under God!"

God makes me giggle, not just sometimes, a lot. God uses the most unlikely people sometimes to do His bidding. For Christians who supported Donald J. Trump, we knew that he was not a choirboy; however, we could see that he was the candidate who promised to uphold Godly principles. The heroes of the Holy Bible are men and women that are not always angels, but with God's help they managed to activate His agenda. America was in deep need of a miracle, and God's plans to enact that challenge could not have been any more entertaining. As I watched God work His magic throughout Trump's campaign, like most Christians, we knew there was no denying that God was also enjoying His victory.

Fools were tripping over themselves to tell us that we were idiots, and that "We the People" and our candidate would lose. We knew that their polls were *fake*! We were told by experts that they were the smart ones, yet they suffered loss after loss. Their words became laughable, as they called us names and mocked us and our boy Trump. The most precious moments, which I relive on YouTube whenever I need a good chuckle, were looking at the loathsome media haters' wide-eyed hysteria as they choked back the tears the night of the 2016 election. It was the sweet justice they deserved, akin to the wrath of God! "Forgive me, Lord, if I sound insensitive," but they had been so merciless and hateful, they could use a humble awakening.

Our God and our religious freedoms had been on attack for decades. We knew that we needed our own personal bully to fight back and help us reclaim our rights. President Trump has done more for religious liberty than any other president in the history of our nation. For a man who had not been known for his spiritual beliefs prior to taking office, it is surprising to all Christians that he has faithfully kept his promises where the First Amendment and our freedom of worship is concerned. And Christians have also been blessed to participate in the National Days of Prayer, which have been held more frequently under President Trump's leadership.

For the last sixty years, President Lyndon B. Johnson effectively silenced pastors and other religious leaders with his Johnson Amendment by holding their message hostage to the Internal Revenue Service. President Trump vowed and consequently ended the Johnson Amendment, opening the doors for freer preaching at the pulpit and God's word to guide the political conversation. Trump has not only been respectful of our religious rights, he himself has grown as a man of prayer and worship. It has been a beautiful journey to witness unfolding before our eyes.

*****

We as Christians know that we must try every day to be better people and respect God's laws. Like the parent in heaven that He is, He wants the best for us and our land. Our Lord will bless us with rich rewards, and He will rebuke us for our own well-being. And His love will endure forever.

*****

My Prayer for our Nation

May God bless America, her government, and her citizens from the dark forces of evil! May God open the eyes and ears of our nation's people to see and hear His voice! May God forgive our past sins and mistakes, as we pray for His will to be done across our great land! May God bless our President Donald J. Trump, his administration, our Supreme Court justices, our congressional rulers, state and local leaders with the peace and wisdom of His Holy Spirit to guide us to return to the beautiful country that we were meant to be! May God unite our American family as one people who love their liberty and believe in justice for all! In Jesus's name! Amen!

POLITICS AND RELIGION

*****

For Prayerful Consideration

"I will hear from heaven and will forgive their sin and heal their land" is what our God promises to those who follow as He commands. Our God repeats similar stories throughout His Bible and in His word. His children who do what He asks and obey His laws are blessed, while nations which turn away from our Lord become crippled with despair. Our God teaches His people, again and again, He is a forgiving God of mercy when we, His children, repent and do His will. So why then do we continue to live in ignorance? Do we think that God will change His mind and the rules that He wants us to live by? We have been given every example over and over throughout biblical history, and yet we do not learn the lessons of our Father. Our pride and our sin prevent us from attaining the peace and joy of His Holy Spirit.

I am sure no matter how I feel, I will get some backlash, but I am willing. What do you think? Can you express yourself freely? For those who are Christians or faith leaders, do you think that when we condone negative behaviors, we become complicit? What would Jesus do or say?

I think that all these conversations are worth having to understand one another and hopefully to work some of these problems in our society out. Our differences need to be handled in a way so that we can all coexist.

CHAPTER 13

The Patriotic Movement

We the people are the rightful masters of both Congress
and the Courts, not to overthrow the Constitution but to
overthrow the men who pervert the Constitution.
—President Abraham Lincoln

It is an incredible time to be alive. People are hungry for truth. Cool people are arising and becoming empowered. We are paying attention, and we have found a new sense of awareness. We are standing up for what is right, and we are informing others. But most importantly, we are joining forces and uniting our country's people "As One."

It has also been a time of fear, hopelessness, and sorrow. We are witnessing a cultural war developing against those who love America by those who have been taught to hate America. These haters of America must learn the truth about this benevolent nation. America has been the most generous country in all the world. We are the country that our ally nations call on first for help in dire situations. We have gone to war to help others. And we have fought within our own land in a civil war to end the evils of slavery.

This societal battle has been brewing by these radicals who have been looking for an excuse to burn and destroy our nation, egged on by a Marxist Leftist regime, which has refused to give

America its peaceful transfer of powers. The Radical Left-Wing politicians have no intention of unifying, while they are not in power. They have taught their base to use upheaval to intimidate the general public into submission, and when patriotic citizens refuse to cower and bow to them, they attack and destroy. As our president, his administrative team and his supporters fight toward peaceful unity, building the Unites States' successes, growing the economy and maintaining national security, the Radical Left's fringe plot and scheme to tear her down. As a Leftist group of anarchist and thugs terrorize and vandalize innocent people, they claim to be justified in their actions. Apparently, they were never taught that two wrongs do not make a right.

It has been proven that some in this group of Radical Leftists have been provoking others toward violence and supplying weapons to harm others and damage properties. They have been paid by wealthy manipulators that benefit politically by their rage and terror. The worthy causes of their peaceful protests become lost because of the louder and more aggressive gang of vandals. And yet both sides, the peaceful protesters and the vicious vandals, do not realize that they have become the victims. They have no idea that they are being used and abused by a corrupt cabal of Democrats, who simply want to demolish the current well-being of our nation, in the hope of garnering more votes in the upcoming election and ultimately regaining their authoritarian regime.

Under the leadership of Barack Obama, almost all control of the government had been taken away from "We the People." We were to have no voice and no longer have a *vote*! It was going exactly as planned! The Deep State of the elite establishment politicians and embedded bureaucrats who filled the Washington DC Swamp were completely entrenched in one-sided partisan politics that remained on the side of Globalism. These corrupt men and women were either being blackmailed for past mistakes or they were bought and paid for by their large donors. Follow the money!

Now think! Do you understand that it was essential for us to have a president who owed nothing to anyone? This man would have to be funded either strictly on his own or by "We the People!" The patriotic movement needed a leader who would be theirs and theirs alone. So now, I am going to take you one thought further, I am purposing that this patriotic movement was every bit as thought out as Obama and his swamp creatures' movement to keep sole control of our nation, ending democracy once and for all. The difference is that Obama's plots and schemes were illegal. His administration and minions were spying on Candidate Trump and his campaign, and after that failed, Obama's criminal enterprise orchestrated a coup against a duly elected President Trump. At the same time, the good guys were forming their own patriotic movement, which was strategizing to regain the power for the citizens and to end the dark web of corruption that had overcome our government and her institutions.

Enter stage right, our hero and fearless leader, Donald J. Trump. To some, he may not have been the likely choice; to others, he was the only choice and to many he was the perfect choice. He knows how to push the prideful and arrogant elitist's buttons, which ultimately exposes them as the vicious tyrants of enslavement that they have become. He is a genius in that way; he has masterfully and purposefully managed to expose every one of them. "We the People" also need to shout out a huge thank you to the entire Trump family because they have been the targets of so much verbal and threatening abuse. For those who respect and honor the Constitution of our Founding Fathers and those who appreciate our American values, principles, and way of life, we will be forever grateful to each member of the Trump family!

You may say, Trump is not heroic. However, this billionaire businessman gave up his cushy lifestyle, and truthfully, his popularity with half the country, to save our proverbial asses! He dodges bullets for us all day every day. I often use an analogy to describe President Trump as a pilot flying a plane. He is very busy doing his job, he wants everything to go smoothly with no turbulence, and he is hoping for a safe landing. All the while, the stewardesses are wildly shooting at him to take over the plane. And when he enlists help from the crew, he finds out that they also have been plotting against him, so he cannot even trust them. We the passengers are Trump's only concern; he knows if the plane goes down, none of us will survive. We may be having a really hard time, trying to figure out what those dumb morons who are shooting at our pilot are thinking, but one thing we know for sure is that it has got to stop. While Trump keeps flying the plane, we must be the ones to fight back against those traitors. President Trump can no longer try to save America on his own, he needs every patriotic American to get in the battle. Americans are resilient and strong! Do not mess with the USA!

Whether you like it or not, the game is on! You can get in and play the game, or you can sit on the sidelines and watch. However, you and I can see that the game will be played as scheduled. So you had better pick your team wisely. If you want to participate, we need you. It is time to be "All In!" It is time for us to "root, root, root" for the home team. Because our opponents' end game is to take America out of the game forever, and they are making sure that we will never be able to play or win the game again. Winning is our only option!

Currently, there are several patriotic groups and movements, which have formed across our nation. There have been religious leaders who have inspired us with an ongoing devotion to praying for our nation. There are several call-in prayer groups that I have enjoyed, such as Michael Ortega's "Strike Force of Prayer." You can find more information and sign up at: www.strikeforceofprayer.com. The power of unified prayer is amazing!

I also belong to Lance Wallnau's Facebook group, and I have attended several of his extreme dream trip events. Lance has inspired his members to actively support our president and the nation. He works to educate and inform his patriotic following with the goal for them to be able to share the knowledge he offers by bringing an awareness to the public. While combatting the current struggles on the political battlefield, he also encourages us to pray in unity, "As One." You can find Lance Wallnau's wonderful educational materials, CDs, DVDs, and books at www.lancewallnau.com.

It started with the Trump Train and evolved to the Q Movement, and there are many groups in between. Some people say that they do not believe the Q Movement is real or they call it a conspiracy theory. Regardless, the message is clear that "We the People" are Q, and we are in this patriotic movement to create an awareness for our families, our friends, and our fellow citizens. Our Q Movement is real, we have real leaders, and we all have the same goals to be guardians of truth and freedom and to keep our Republic safe from those who wish to steal our American Dream. For more information regarding the Q Movement, please take some time to watch the first video documentary, which you can currently find on YouTube, it is: Q - Plan to Save the World | WWG1WGA.

*****

Stay tuned as we dig deeper into the strategies of the patriotic movement sweeping the nation free of the crime and corruption in our government bureaucracies and Deep State.

Trust the plan and stay the course!

The storm is upon us!

WWG1WGA!

Beware! They Will Be Out to Get You!

Freedom is never more than one generation away from extinction. We didn't pass it to our children in the bloodstream. It must be fought for, protected, and handed on for them to do the same.
—Ronald Reagan

In the moment you become blissfully aware, it is an enlightening to your spirit. A feeling of revelation comes over you because you have uncovered the truth. Excitement fills your body as you unfold more details, and suddenly, you have been illuminated with an understanding of the value of what you have received. You may experience reoccurring heartfelt emotions as you discover that the truth should have been obvious to you all along. Suddenly, you may be inspired to share your newfound knowledge with those you love, and if you are, the powerful words that you need to communicate will come upon you. A stirring in your soul may motivate you to bravely share the valuable treasures which you have discerned. The importance of the cherished evidence that you have revealed gives you the bravery needed to reach out to others so that they can become aware, too. Being a beacon of light that shines in a dark place is a worthy endeavor! America has been suffering through some dark places lately. When we go through bitter struggles, it is crucial that we do not become bitter ourselves instead fight the bitter times with acts of love and kindness by sharing the truth as a ray of light in its darkness. The dire consequences of the choices we make as a nation in this moment are too important to the futures of our children and grandchildren. We must actively get involved. Bravely awaken those around you so that together, we can save the destiny of our land, which is the unity, freedom, liberty, and justice that she has promised!

Hell hath no fury like a Far Left-Wing Liberal! Their Resistance and Antifa Radicals have lost their blooming minds, and they are trying to take us with them. Some people call it Trump derangement syndrome, but whatever it is, it is not rational or as Michelle Obama considers herself "becoming."

If you voted for Donald Trump, they have punished you, financially and spiritually. Unless you do their bidding, you are of no concern to them. Cower, grovel, get on your knees, and above all else, do not dare disagree with these extreme activists. Fight back and "Beware! They will be out to get you!"

It has been determined that Trump won a fair election in 2016. And in my opinion, he would have won by a larger margin if there had been no cheating on the Democratic side. For those of us that were Trump supporters, we were happy and excited after he won, and we wanted to rejoice. Many of us from the Trump Train were very disappointed to be made to curb our enthusiasm. Some of us were even physically prevented from getting to our celebrations by an angry mob. The silence from the mainstream media was deafening as no coverage of the violent destruction coming from the Antifa agitators was televised. On Fox News shows with commentators like Tucker Carlson, Judge Jeanine Pirro, Hannity, and Lou Dobbs, you could find the truth, and you would have seen the aggressive protesters burning the limousine of a fellow patriot, physically attacking people with bloody violence, the breaking of windows, and the destruction of property. These anarchists are not loving, kind, provoked, abused, or mistreated, as projected by the Liberal media. They simply did not get their way, and they were going to make sure that those who did would suffer by their abusive and evil tactics.

Hell hath no fury like a Women's March activist! "Love Trumps Hate" were the hypocritical words of those who claim to be the tolerant ones. *Love* is a word that they have no intention of using toward anyone who does not think like they do, and they are the furthest thing from tolerant. These odd women do not speak for me or my women pals. My Trump-loving lady friends would not dress up in ugly pink hats or, even worse, as a vagina, marching around spewing hateful rhetoric, while claiming to be pillars of virtue. "Becoming" women give others the right to their own choice and behave appropriately. We sucked it up when Obama won in both 2008 and 2012. We did not accuse him falsely, and we did not wallow in a hatred for him or even self-pity. No, we patiently waited our turn and accepted our fate, even though we did not agree with it or think that it was in our best interests.

Thug-like tactics, sometimes laced with verbal and/or physical intimidation, have become their alterative to reasonable communication. They reject the truth because they have been taught to hate patriotism. These misled souls have been saturated in anti-American doctrine and rhetoric, which offers a selfish and racist view of those of us who love the country we share. Many of these manipulated Liberals have no idea that they have been deceived, so they attack you rather than let you defend yourself. The more you resist their false narrative, the more fervently they resist, and their attacks against you become uglier and louder. The most extreme will accuse you of what they themselves are guilty of. Hate hoaxes are a masterful game of the Left-Wing Radicals. They may falsely accuse you while they violently bloody you or destroy your property. And the more truth you share or credible that you appear, it makes them either seethe with greater rage or have a total ballistic meltdown. This irrational group must be taught that their entitled upbringing will not to be condoned.

We should also understand that sometimes when we present the truth or facts, we run the risk of dealing with a Liberal who has been told that Conservatives threaten their lifestyle. And although we know this is not accurate, it does not change the belief system and conditioning of the mind-set of the far Left-Winger. It is hard to hold an intelligent or open-minded conversation with someone who has preconceived notions about the person with whom they are speaking. It is never easy when you or the person that you are communicating with feels defensive. People will sometimes react in unflattering ways when they feel attacked. Our goal of trying to reason with the opposing Radical Liberal or Anarchist will most like fall on deaf ears. And sometimes even trying to listen to them is met with much difficulty because they may still see you as posing a threat.

On the flip side, not all Democrats have gone blooming mad, a majority are great people. There are some very reasonable and levelheaded Liberals. They are compassionate and they have good intentions. My heart goes out to them right now in this current wild political scene. Those rational Democrats do have a true desire for the well-being of our nation and her people. Some of them have not bought into the lies and manipulation, and they can see that their political party has gone off the rails. For those who are waking up to the dangerous tactics of their Left-Wing agitators, we can only hope that they can reign their comrades in. Civil Rights Attorney Leo Terrell has become a wonderful and articulate voice on the Left, and we can only hope that clearheaded minds like his will prevail. Our common goals are to make the public aware of the shrewd political strategies that have ignited this waging cultural war and ways in which we can avoid the division that they cause. And through it all, we must manage to remain friendly throughout our struggles when expressing the differences in our opinions.

As a talent manager for over the past fifteen years, I have been working with some of the most hostel outspoken Liberals. Some have been actors, who are my clients, and some have been the casting directors, who cast my actors in television shows, commercials and major film projects. I never realized how quiet I must remain when it came to my political opinions because those with whom I was working were so open with their Liberal thoughts. I have seen some of them use the most vile and hateful language coming from the other side. I have witnessed my business colleagues lie, use gross language, and make filthy misrepresentations of President Trump and his family members. Like most of us, I enjoy using the ever-biased Facebook and Twitter, but holy cow, the moment I posted a positive story about our president, I got flooded with concerns from my Liberal talent. They would ask me, for the fear of being blacklisted, "Please do not post your Conservative views or any favoritism toward our president."

I committed myself to *only* posting loving and kind material, which was fine with me regardless. However, I was very surprised that even if I was speaking well of someone on the Conservative side of the aisle, I was still lambasted. My response in any defense of the positive story would be met with such negative feedback. As rage and anger was spewed at me, I found my professional obligation to my clients was unfairly keeping me silent while they themselves were vile and disgusting. The final injustice for me was my inability to defend what I knew were cruel deceptions. Until recently, when I suddenly decided that justice sometimes comes by the form of a rather harsh rebuke, and in the end, your reward is through the benefit of others, with their awareness which may bring them out of their hate-filled fog.

Boycotting and blackballing businesses and rallying others to do the same because you differ in your thinking on political issues may seem unusually cruel. However, there are times that it may be appropriate and effective. Some manufacturers and store owners publicly fund operations based on their political leanings, and if those causes align with yours, you may choose to buy products from those companies. The opposite would be for you to not pay for items from a business which donates to a foundation that you find moral reprehensible. And if a company owner should voice an opinion that is tarnished with lies or causes pain, it might turn your stomach to support a business funding such corrupted viewpoints. The bottom line is that there are bullies in the business world who may choose to show favoritism and bias when you react to the differing opinions of those around you. Those bullies intend to control you with their masterful manipulation. Beware and be strong because they may be out to get you!

THE PATRIOTIC MOVEMENT

*****

Jew and Gentile, we are one nation under God. Black and White, we are one nation indivisible. Democrat and Republican, we are all Americans.
—President Ronald Reagan on July 4, 1986

Our fight must be a unifying one! The battle is not with the Liberals or Democrats, who are the unwitting victims of the powerful schemes of the dark cabal of wealthy elitists and the corrupt Deep State politicians. And it is not actually a quarrel with one political party or the other. We are simply patriotic individuals who have recognized that we run the risk of losing our sovereignty as a nation and the freedoms and rights that go with it. We can no longer trust those who we elect to rule. And we are not alone. Cool people all over the world are witnessing the dismantling of their countries, too. We all are in this global effort to end the oppressive regimes. This is bigger than anything that we could have imagined, and we never dreamed that we may be on the side of the good guys, rising to save the free nations of the earth.

When you trap the demons, they unleash their fury. They are not nice, like us. They do not play fair. They are wicked, and they have no shame in making you suffer. They will take you down at all costs. President Trump and the patriots stopped their evil plans, and they loathe us. They need to make their minions loathe us, too, and when they cannot, their wrath becomes a bitter revenge. Their extreme resistance does not offer us the ability to share this country we love. As they keep doubling down in their reign of terror, they continue to lose repeatedly. As we win, win, win, it makes them lose their minds even further!

The patriots and Trump know that we have only *one* choice at this point, and that is to bring down the hammer of justice! Draining the swamp is the only way we all can survive this wicked plot that has been ravaging on our nation. And by cleaning up the corruption, we may finally be able to end the evil, which has caused the cultural war of division between goodhearted Americans. Victory is crucial because they will kill and destroy anyone or anything that gets in their way. Our President Trump was so right when he stepped back for a moment, knowing that he was ripe for the set up that he saw coming from the Radical Left, and he spoke the words, "Sometimes you just need to let people *see* for themselves, instead of trying to warn them."

The storm is upon us!

CHAPTER 14

Uniting as One Nation

E Pluribus Unum
Latin for "Out of many, one."

In 2001, following the 9/11 attack, there was a public service announcement with several ethnically diverse people saying, "I am an American."

After the screen fades to black, the Latin words "E Pluribus Unum" appear with the English translation beneath, reading, "Out of many, one."

It was a powerful message of true patriotism. We should let that sink in for a minute. We are one family, as Americans. That one word unites us, we are all Americans! We share in something beautiful, and it is our bond!

I would prefer that we no longer separate ourselves with a hyphen. What say you? A hyphen separates us from our common bond. However, if you choose to use a hyphen, please do not let it isolate you from your identity as an American.

The words patriot and American have no certain skin color or gender!

Nothing unites people as quickly as a tragic event. During the saddest of times, people come together with a heartfelt love, driven by their shared compassion for one another. We are seeing it now with the coronavirus that has plagued our nation and the world. The American people truly followed the protocol that was set before them, by staying in as requested. Care providers, nurses, doctors, emergency personnel risked their health daily by looking after those who were suffering from the illness. Younger people honorably looked out for their elderly family and neighbors by going out of their way help others. When you were able to go out, you could see people not only respecting each other's space but wearing masks and gloves. The sacrifices were endless, and most Americans have joined in the effort willingly, with a spirit of caution and unity.

In this chapter, I would like to discuss a call to action. The goal of this action is the patriotic unity of the citizens, who share this great nation. Some of you may respond with no interest to participate at all, others may have little interest, and the remainder may be fully on board. Whatever your level of engagement, it is nice to be aware and positive. My hope is that a large part of you will feel, as I do, that you are being purposefully placed in a position to change the course of this country for the benefit and well-being of yourself, your children, your grandchildren, and your neighbors. So let us join forces for a better America!

I am going to ask that you set aside your differences. Do not think politically, as a Democrat, Republican, Liberal, or Conservative. Be colorblind and gender neutral. Do not squabble out the social issues! They are important, but they are not more important than our love for one another and America. No longer let those radical bullies of Hollywood, the mainstream media, and our corrupt ruling class intimidate you with the fear of speaking up for what is right and what is the truth. Those instigators of division are the *privileged*! We are not the privileged. Those powerful elitists will try to convince you that we are the ones offending others, when in all honesty, they simply what to provoke us. Be bold, strong, and brave! It is time to take their power away, and give it back where it belongs, in the hands of "We the People!"

Healing the Nation

> *When America is united, America is totally unstoppable.*
> —Donald Trump

As mentioned previously, President George Washington was greatly opposed to having separate political parties. He thought that it would divide the nation. However, in the early 1790s, Thomas Jefferson and Alexander Hamilton formed two groups, the Republicans and the Federalists (now known as the Democrats). Could you imagine if we could simply be the American Party? What if we no longer knew if a politician had a (R) or a (D) next to their name? Do you sometimes vote for someone solely by the (R) or the (D)? What if we all became Independents? What if we took the time to know our representatives? And what if we could hold them to their campaign promises or give them the boot? I am not sure if we can get there; however, I think that it is worth a try. Let us follow the advice of our first president, as we get back to the founding principles that made America beautiful, by unifying the political parties to be one. And in the words of our beloved President Abraham Lincoln, we should aspire to restore our country to its rightful owners, as a "government of the people, by the people, for the people!"

"We the People" can inspire others to find ways to make our country peaceful and united regardless of our age, race, creed, gender, or political party, with the goal of ending any divisions that have been forced upon us by selfish politicians. We the citizens of these United States had better wake up before it is too late. The awareness starts when we realize that we have been manipulated by these greedy and power-mongering politicians, who thrive on dividing us to benefit their political agendas. They have only one goal, and that is garnering our votes. Knowing this is what gives the power back to the American people. And helping others understand this is what will ultimately heal our nation.

Friends do not let their friends be bamboozled! I am going to encourage you to reach out, as a good shepherd would, in a loving and caring way, to make a difference, one lost sheep or flock at a time.

It is going to take respectful dialogue, speaking the truth, defending our stances, setting the record straight, and a lot of listening to one another. Ask questions! Hear and pay attention! Speak about each other's feelings and truly sympathize with their answers. Be articulate, respectful, and kind, and ask for the same in return.

What can we do? How can we stop the nonsense? As I have pointed out in previous chapters, wittingly the generous hearted Liberals have watched as their Democratic Party has been kidnapped and taken over by Radicals. They are no longer the party of John F. Kennedy, who said, "Conformity is the jailer of freedom and the enemy of growth."

I believe that JFK would have disagreed with the attitudes of the Radical Left, who expect you to conform to their demands or they will crucify your character, violently intimidate you, and/or damage your property. He further elaborated with "Only an educated and informed people will be a free people."

John F. Kennedy was assassinated on November 22, 1963. There has always been speculation about his death. And I hope that one day we will learn the truth. JFK had made some corrupt politicians very nervous with his statement, "I will splinter the Central Intelligence Agency into a thousand pieces and scatter it into the wind."

You see, in the 1950s, the Central Intelligence Agency (CIA) started an operation called Mockingbird. This put in motion their plan to manipulate and use the mainstream media, radio, and American journalism to influence the public by swaying their ideology for the CIA's political and social benefit. Project Mockingbird was, as the word suggests, repeated words and ideas to brainwash our society. In 1975, the CIA admitted to these tactics being used on everyday citizens of both subliminal and direct messaging as a form of persuasion. They still do this today. And if you become aware of these shrewd practices, the CIA would use the term "conspiracy theorist" to attack you or anyone who questioned their governmental secrets. However, the truth is never a conspiracy!

Some of JFK's last words that ring true in the current political environment were "Those who make peaceful revolution impossible will make violent revolution inevitable."

Thus, the party of JFK no longer exists, and many Democrats are finally waking up to this fact. Even if only 10 to 20 percent of our countrymen have been brainwashed into becoming unhinged Liberals, that 10 to 20 percent has grabbed the loudest microphone. So it is time for the rational Americans to take that microphone away from them and use it ourselves to restore our country to her former glory. I urge you to join me in whatever capacity you can. I am challenging you to become a political activist for the USA, one step at a time and with as much or as little effort as you can. Please become a member of the patriotic movement that we have started across the nation to end the political divide and unite our citizens.

Since we have learned the strategies in the Radical Liberals' and swamp creatures' playbook, we can use their tactics against them by making their blinded victims aware of their dishonest and divisive games. Now, I am not going to suggest that we lie and cheat in the same way they do, but instead, change the game altogether to one of truth and integrity so they cannot help but lose. Naysayers say that it is too late to end this current cultural war of hatred toward one another, and those "doom and gloomers" believe it is an impossible task. However, they are wrong, and we are up to the challenge!

For those of us who are Christians, we know that our God is the Way, the Truth, and the Life. Our enemy is Satan, who is a masterful liar. We must know our power is through Him who makes all things possible. And we must trust in God's gifts of the Holy Spirit, among which offer us the gift of wisdom, knowledge, and understanding. We need the power of prayer and the help of a God who loves us. And He loves America!

*****

So as in Ephesians 6:10–18,

Finally, be strong in the Lord and in His mighty power. Put on the full armor of God, so that you can take your stand against the devil's schemes. For our struggle is not against flesh and blood, but against rulers, against the authorities, against the powers of this dark world and against the spiritual forces of evil in the heavenly realms.

Therefore, put on the full armor of God, so that when the day of evil comes, you may be able to stand your ground, and after you have done everything, to stand. Stand firm then, with the belt of truth buckled around your waist, with the breastplate of righteousness in place, and with your feet fitted with the readiness that comes from the gospel of peace. In addition to all this, take up the shield of faith, with which you can extinguish all the flaming arrows of the evil one. Take the helmet of salvation and the sword of the Spirit, which is the word of God.

And pray in the Spirit on all occasions with all kinds of prayers and requests. With this in mind, be alert and always keep on praying for all the Lord's people. (NIV)

*****

As we have determined previously, the Republican Party has also become entrenched in corruption. They have many swamp creatures dwelling in their party, too. Some are establishment elite, some are "Never Trumpers," and some are what we call RINOs (Republicans in Name Only). However, with all that said, the Republican Party most closely lines up with our golden opportunity to gain control of America again. Therefore, building on the party of President Trump and finding loyalists within that party will be the safest road to travel in getting us to where we are headed. "We the People" can make some adjustments along the way.

There are many ways that we can be a positive influence to heal the wounds and calm the fears of Americans who have been misled by the political elites and their corrupt allies. One of the ways is to create a dialogue with easy questions, such as, "Are you painfully aware that something needs to change? If you thought that you could make a positive difference, would you? Would you like to see peace and unity, although we have different ideas?"

Once we open a thoughtful conversation, ask for the respectful treatment that you require. Suggest that you both can share your ideas freely and speak of your feelings without any anger or condemnation of one another. Share things that you have in common and refer to those things often throughout your discussion.

Develop a Game Plan

> *Let us not seek the Republican answer or the Democratic answer,*
> *but the right answer. Let us not seek to fix the blame for the*
> *past. Let us accept our own responsibility for the future.*
> —John F. Kennedy

Many of our friends and family members may wish to never speak about the politics of the day. You can truly see why they would not because the environment is so contentious. They might like to spend their free time sitting by the pool, sipping a cocktail and remaining blissfully unaware. None of us relish the idea of a verbal debate that may turn hostile. It takes a special kind of passion to tackle the existing problems around us. Recognizing the need is the first motivating factor; however, a love for America is the inspiration behind the desire to get on the frontlines of this ensuing battle. At this moment in our history, we will be known as the patriotic warriors who saved the American Dream!

As you create a strategy for yourself, figure out where your talent can be best utilized and determine your level of contribution to the cause. Please feel free to look at what I have mapped out for myself, to be a part of this patriotic movement. My intention was to give you a chance to examine your feelings and thoughts and to assist you in finding a direction that you would choose to consider for yourself. "Good teachers do not inspire followers they inspire good teachers."

*****

Below, I have listed the purposes of this book, which I hope you have been able to benefit from. Please feel free to share with others.

- To help us become aware and figure out ways to generate an awareness in those unwitting souls around us. To grow an understanding of the ongoing problems, which have been dividing our citizens, and recognizing that they are not our fault. Exposing the truth that the hate, rage, and confusion that we are witnessing are coming intentionally from the swamp creatures of the Washington DC Deep State within our dishonest ruling class. These long-serving shady politicians, bureaucrats, and their deceptive allies in the mainstream media and Hollywood must be exposed for their roles in the chaos which has been ensuing. Our goal is to combat this corruption and end it once and for all!

- To generate an open communication between our citizens, regardless of our social and political views. Inspiring us to find ways to make our country peaceful!

- To take away the blame and shame that have been inflicted on "We the People" and place it squarely where it belongs on the perpetrators of the lies and malicious schemes which divide us and keep us weak. To promote reasonable debate and thought-provoking dialogue. To urge freethinkers to express themselves rationally!

- To encourage readers to join across our diverse nation, to embrace each other's differences and coexist for our mutual benefit, for the futures of our children and grand-children. To "unhyphenate" our culture and become simply Americans! We are to be, as our Pledge of Allegiance states, "One nation under God, indivisible with liberty and justice for *all*."

- To help you and to teach you to help others to become discerning of the manipulative words and behaviors of those in areas of influence that have left our society blinded, brainwashed, and misled because of the destructive false narratives they propagate. To advance truth seeking and fact-finding methods!

- To gather the passionate patriot group! To merge these national movements of Americans who are fighting to save the country from those who wish to destroy her! In their effort to keep our sovereignty, liberty, Constitution, and the Bills of Rights! For the sake of the unity of our righteous citizens, "We the People" voting to save our sacred American Dream!

*****

The goals that I set for my book and myself may not be of interest to you; however if they are, feel free to use them as a guideline. Regardless of your ability to commit or the level of involvement you may desire, your individual awareness is a step in the success of the patriot's mission statement. Even after I woke up, so to speak, throughout my research for this project, I have been stunned by new and shocking realities. And continually, we all are finding more revelations unfolding before our very eyes.

Research is going to be the key in your awareness and your ability to inform others. Now remember, truth and factual evidence to back it up are going to be required for patriots to counter the negative press, the misinformed social media trolls, and those who have been fooled and blinded for so long. We always need to find trusted sources. I have complied a list of the information outlets that I have been enjoying for updates and news. You can find those details in my "Resources and Networking" page toward the end of the book. However, with every resource that I follow, I question everything that I hear and see, and I hope that you would do the same. Then, listen to your conscience, your intuition can give you a keen sense of foreboding or an astute thrill of awakening.

Identifying the enemies of "We the People" is crucial! You must understand who your enemies are, so you can plan your counterattack. It may sound harsh to use the term "*enemy*"; however, these are people who have indoctrinated our children intentionally to use them for their malicious deeds, so the word "*enemy*" is mild comparatively speaking. We need to be bold and brave; this is not a time to back down. And while we can be beacons of light in the darkness, we also may need to intensely rebuke those who wish us and our fellow patriots harm. I want to touch upon the standard that I have set for myself, but you can determine your own ethical code and behavior. For myself, those who are the evil and wicked perpetrators of the injustice which has divide the people of the nation, receive no soft words from me. They receive my salty rebuke! However, when it comes to the *unwitting* trolls of the Radical Left, I try my best to win them over with rational dialogue. You may say that it is hopeless, but I remain ever hopeful that they are not a lost cause. I truly care for individuals that have been the victims of a demonic hypnotizing cult. We, on the other hand, are the purveyors of the truth and the seekers of unity and inclusion, so we must never lower our standards to the level of the enemy by using lies or name-calling profanities.

Join one or some of the patriotic movements and then recruit and encourage others to become members, too. Growing our patriotic movements and merging them together is going to be our key to public awareness. There are so many new organizations in which to participate, including prayer groups, that have formed across our nation with the common goals, of American sovereignty and unity for "We the People." We need to help others understand that although some of these clubs may be labeled Conservative or Republican, and they may not be perfectly aligned with the entire country's views, those groups align themselves with a strict adherence to the Constitution and founding principles of the US government. The Grand Ole Party can help patriots to our goal of reclaiming our American Dream and giving power back to "We the People." Although the Republican Party has needed an overhaul, in the recent past, they seem to have made a wonderful start by embracing President Trump's America First political agenda, and you can see them trending toward "We the People." Even our moderate Democrat friends should agree with us, it is time for our nation to come together and cease the power from the corrupt Washington DC Swamp and give it back to American citizens where it belongs.

You may want to form your own group and invite members. Underlining themes of any club should be to grow the patriotic movement, and to maintain a positive message of unity. Invite your friends to participate in gatherings, and ask them to invite their friends. Be inclusive! Have greeters who welcome and introduce members. Encourage fun activities and more participation within the club's people. Attend other club's and group's meetings, to network and get to know one another. Ask for referrals. Hold membership drives, with the intentions of spreading positive messages to achieve awareness and include everyone. Use your groups to promote fund-raising for worthy causes.

By using social media as a tool, we have a huge resource to reach out to others and share information. Create websites and make accounts with Facebook, Twitter, Parler, Instagram, YouTube, and other social media pages for yourself and your groups, then invite new friends and followers. Rule #1! Do not be angry and do not raise your voice with any kind of intimidation. No name-calling! We are in the business of making friends, we do not want to be one of the crazy Radicals that we are preaching against. Even if they hurl insults at you, be confident and firm, and know that you are on the right side of the political game and the right side of history. Do not retreat from the digital battlefield that you are using to fulfill your mission. In fact, all of us should have multiple back-up accounts, in case we become victims of the biased censorship that has been used as an attack on patriots. Who would think we are living on the edge? LOL! I do not consider myself a threat or even a radical. Dang, I am just a Conservative church lady! That used to be a good thing, an upstanding citizen. But I am no longer clutching my pearls in fear. (Not that, I ever really did. ☺) Yikes! Now, we are considered extremists. Well, if they can terminate or suspend my Facebook or Twitter pages, I am ready with back up accounts under their platforms. I have made sure to have accounts with Parler and Instagram, too. And I hope that you will do the same.

Rev up your influence base by promoting your pages and accounts daily. Network, mingle, connect, "Like," comment, invite, share, and support fellow patriots in their battle on their pages and sites. It is critical that "where we go one, we go all." Be a patriotic team and play together, "As One!" We will rise or fall united! This is a crucial time to dispute all the false stories floating around these social media platforms; do not simply ignore the lies and propaganda, we must fight back with the truth. Our president is a counterpuncher, and he is winning. We need to follow his lead and be counterpunchers, too. President Trump has referred to the silent war that has been raging, and he is correct. It is a cultural war, and much of it has been being fought out on a digital battlefield. This information warfare is vital to how we move forward as a nation and throughout the world. Truth warriors need to get in the movement of good against evil to save humanity and the freedoms we all love! Together we can win!

If you hear or see a lie, ask for the proof to back it up. Use counter questions that make them think. Challenge those who attack with deceit, make them prove their statements, and then smack them down with the truth. They like to say that Trump lies all the time; ask them to name three lies. I have not had one person come up with anything other than a lie that they had been told. They do not expect you to ask for details about their fibs. It is hysterical watching them bumble all over themselves realizing in fear that they must answer with facts. Remember, most of the Trump haters are unaware that they are lying because they have gotten their lies (that they assume are the truth) from the liars who fed them to them from the *fake* news outlets. Also, there is nothing wrong with you responding that you had heard the opposite of their lie to counter their false narrative. For example, I had several liberal friends say it was horrible that Trump would lock kids in cages, and they would show me the photos. If you know the facts, those photos were from when Obama was the president, and those were his policies. You could simply reply, "Wow, that is amazing, I heard that actually happened under the Obama's administration. And those photos are from his policies at the border."

Sometimes, we do not want to argue with a friend or family member, but if we truly care about them and our country, we cannot let them be filled with the vicious bogus stories that turn them into haters. We are compassionate and loving when we take the time to care enough to dispute the brutal salacious propaganda, they have been hearing and seeing.

When you take on this patriotic mission, you are being enlisted to help and serve your community and your country. Organize your day so that you can take time to be an inspirational influencer with the truth and be a positive role model for those who need hope and encouragement. Connect with people and connect people to other patriotic people. Continually share resources and true news updates.

We are extremely blessed to have some amazing and dynamic black Conservatives, who have not only woke, but they are speaking out. They have formed a Blexit movement. These superstars include Candace Owens, Terrence K. Williams, CJ Pearson, Diamond and Silk, Brandon Tatum, David J. Harris Jr., The Hodgetwins, Black Conservative Patriot, the Right Brothers, Lawrence Jones, Star Parker, Joel Patrick, Larry Elder, and so many more excellent role models. These courageous Americans are such wonderful clear-thinking, articulate voices for the patriotic movement sweeping the nation. Let them do your speaking for you! Follow and support them on social media and, most important, share their posts and videos. Also, make sure to share the #walkaway video testimonies from former Democrats and Liberals by Brandon Straka. You can find him on most social media platforms.

Support the Conservative or Patriotic politicians on social media and make financial donations, if you can. "We the People" need to have full control of the House of Representative and the Senate to pass Trump's agenda in putting America first. They will help him in the fight against the corrupt Deep State of establishment politicians and bureaucrats. These patriotic candidates will show up and back President Trump in his efforts to Make America Great!

Get reliable information from alternative news outlets, which are available on some of the cable networks, such as, OAN is One America Network, CBN is Christian Broadcasting Network, and News Max. They are all great sources with trusted new reporting. YouTube also has patriotic news sources such as Just Informed, And We Know, The X22 Report, Woke Societies, The Officer Tatum, Just the News, Jennifer Mac, Black Conservative Patriot, Steel Truth,

Lance Wallnau, Judicial Watch, The Patriot Hour, and so many more. And I highly recommend searching for Juan O' Savin's interviews on YouTube, especially his chats with Jennifer Mac, you will get a treasure trove of important details to prepare you for the upcoming events. You choose who you enjoy and trust to give you the truth and *real* news! And when it comes to a great national newspaper, I love the *Epoch Times*. It is such a wonderful newspaper with great content.

Truth seekers need fact-based resources that they can trust. Be sure to research on your own and find reliable people who have no hidden agendas. And make sure when you spread the word, that you are giving *real* news!

Support patriotic clubs on campuses; financial donations are a blessing to these young people's groups. Millennials are our future! These monetary contributions can be personal and/or from your groups. Invite young people to attend your club meetings. And have charismatic patriotic speakers, who present strong content and inspirational topics.

Churches are starting to "get it!" I am loving Calvary Chapel in Chino Hills, California. They are a nondenominational Christian church. They have wonderful music, and Pastor Jack Hibbs gives inspiration instruction in his sermons. I found Calvary Church online during the shutdown period of the coronavirus, and it was a true blessing to be able to watch their services online. They offer great hope, education, and encouragement reflecting on these biblical times in which we are living. You can find them on Facebook or at their website: https://calvarycch.org/

Church leaders are understanding that by being complacent about the nation's problems, they are not supporting Godly principles and their congregations. The church must take a role in our communities and our nation for the sake of God's people and His word. Reach out to pastors and Bible study leaders in your churches. Ask them about the possibility of starting political discussion groups within your churches. Find out if the church has a 501c3 tax exempt status and ask if it affects the pastors' and Bible leaders' ability to use free speech regarding political debate in your churches. There are few gray areas any longer for Christians when it comes to political policies, social stances, and our politicians. What used to be touchy political subjects are now religious issues that need to be decided and supported by the church and its members. Vote for candidates and propositions that align themselves squarely with God and His word.

Start prayer groups, Bible studies, and/or micro churches to educate and pray for our country and our leaders. Many people have opened their homes for such meetings. Some Christian believers have made live and taped videos to inspire their faith communities. And you can create prayer line conference calls, too. All wonderful ways to promote continued awareness, along with the amazing power of prayer. As Jesus words tell us in Matthew 18:20, "For where two or three gathers in my name, there am I with them" (NIV).

Supporting family entertainment is crucial in our battle to limit Hollywood's influence on our youth and society. There are some wonderful streaming services. I enjoy Pure Flix. Watching and promoting Christian films and supporting Christian production companies is important to combat Hollywood's grip on our culture.

Boycott the mainstream media and speak up about their lies and deception by countering their false narratives with the truth. Watch and share Prager University (Prager U) videos; you can get them on YouTube. They offer honest documentaries that give you solid facts and guide you in a logical way to understand the frustrations of our current cultural war.

Simply have the conversation! Do not let your loved ones get blindsided. Be informed and inform others. Invite a friend, family member, or a few people over for tea and politics. Enjoy some wine or beer and have some bar room talk about politics. If you know Democrats that enjoy talking about the current political turmoil in a reasonable way, invite them for a respectful conversation. Before you meet, prepare your talking points. If you are shy, rehearse and even memorize some of the views you would like to share. During the conversation, ask questions and really listen before speaking. Be thoughtful by bringing up matters that you agree upon and then be prepared to defend your patriotic viewpoints, which benefit all of us. And even if your ideology sways to the Left Wing, that is all right because always remember, our mission is to regain control of our government and get it out of the hands of corrupt politicians. Got it? Our issues are not about black or white, gay or straight, life or choice, gun or no guns, immigration, etc. Our goals are to unite Americans and together reclaim our nation!

*****

In all the strategies that I have listed above, remember to have your facts and prepare your talking points. If you are speaking with a staunch anti-Trumper, they will not be open to your adoration of him. Be honest about some of the things that you wish President Trump would do differently; it will loosen the mood of the conversation, and the listener will not assume that you are under some magical spell. Trump is human, just like the rest of us, and he makes mistakes. Be honest about his imperfections because it will create a mutual respect with those with whom you are sharing your thoughts. Just remember, your intention is not to create an argument.

I read all President Trump's tweets, Facebook posts, and watch his rallies and interviews. Most of the time, he is awesome and a true genius. I truly love him! He is delightful, charming, funny, and his attractive smile gets me every time! However, I am not stupid, I have often said, "I wish he could just let some things go."

He is the president, the ruler of the free world, he does not need to give some jerks and bozos the time of day. They hate him! They are ugly green monsters, who are consumed with jealousy! He has gotten under their skin, but he does not need to let them get under his. I wish I could have five minutes to coach him. Yes! This humble average everyday woman would love to be his forgotten woman adviser. Because we, forgotten men and women, have a lot to offer!

Be strong! Be proud! Defend with integrity! State the truth about Conservative values and policies with confidence and love!

CHAPTER 15

Covfefe

is an antediluvian term meaning, "In the end we win!"

In the great words of President Donald Trump "Despite the constant negative press *covfefe*."

My, how the fake news media went out of their minds. You would have thought Trump blew up the White House. He certainly blew up Twitter.

The speculations about what the president meant or the mistake he had made were hysterical. The tweet went out six minutes after midnight (EDT) on May 31, 2017, and it became the obsession of the next week. The most logical assumption was that Trump had misspelled the word "coverage." The Liberal haters were sure he was losing his mental stability, or so they were hoping. Some thought it was meant to be "coffee," others were sure it was meant to be "coverage," and some suspected it was simply a bizarre typo. Even President Trump joined in the fun by tweeting out, "Who can figure out the true meaning of covfefe? Enjoy!"

Fifteen hours later, in a press conference, White House Press Secretary Sean Spicer was asked about the tweet. And he managed to drive the mainstream media and journalists into an even greater frenzy with his classic response, "The president and a small group of people know exactly what he meant."

Covfefe is an ancient biblical term meaning, "In the end we win," and it was used against the evil actions of those who had led men astray. Whether President Trump meant to use the word "Covfefe" as it was truly intended, isn't the prophetic significance stunning. Referring to the negative press as those who lead men astray is so appropriate. In other words, "Despite those who lead men astray, in the end, 'We the People' win."

CONCLUDING NOTE
FROM THE AUTHOR

D ear Reader,
This note is for you, if you made it through my entire book without burning it. And if you passed it on to your friends and family, an even greater kudos to *you*!

I appreciate your patience with my feisty ranting, at times, and I apologize for my provocative dialogue. Some words are just too perfect! And no other words have their impact or meaning. I am forever grateful for your willingness to understand my frustrations within the current political environment. And whether you feel the same way or not, I am truly blessed to be on this rocky patriotic journey with *you*!

For those of you who do not share my views, through reading these pages, I hope that you can now see that we all can only coexist if we tolerate each other's opinions and stop condemning one another for having them. If we honestly want what is best for our nation and the world, we must stop jumping to conclusions with preconceived notions and end the personal attacks. However, we should never accept corruption or treasonous acts, and we all must expose the lies and deception. Let us flip those false narratives upside down and unite our country once and for all!

Thank you for this chance to share my thoughts with you!
May God bless America and the world! And may God bless *you*!
With love,
Julia

CONCLUDING NOTE FROM THE AUTHOR

PS: Please get this book to that pathetic loser, Hillary Clinton. So at last she will know what happened. She should be having some free time very soon!

ACKNOWLEDGMENTS

I have been so blessed to have had the support of my wonderful husband, Tom Parmeter, who has given me the freedom, opportunity, and time that I have needed to take to complete this book project. Thank you for your unending sacrifice to the cause and for agreeing with me. (Well! On the contents of the book anyway! ☺)!

To my two daughters, Lacey and Rachel, thank you for your patience with me during this long process and for your amazing encouragement. You both make me so proud, and I love you more than you know!

Everyone loves my mother, Helen Burris! She is a living breathing saint! She always hated when we would say that, but it is the truth. Mom, you have made me always want to be a better person. You have been my greatest fan, when I desperately needed one, but didn't deserve one. And you have been the person that I would run to first for any guidance. I love you!

Not everyone has a special angel to watch over them when they are writing a book, however, I do. My beloved stepmother, Barbara Peters, may be in heaven, but she is with me in spirit. We were truly likeminded in our Conservative Christian feelings and love for politics. When I started this book, she helped to reinforce my desire, and when I said I couldn't, she said I could. She offered her words to intermingle with mine and fill a few of these pages, and I know that she has been by my side, giving me the inspiration that I have needed to keep going.

ACKNOWLEDGMENTS

Thank you to my father, Bill Peters, who has loyally assisted me throughout my life's endeavors. You have given me the courage to aim a little higher and have the faith needed to succeed.

I must give a special mention of appreciation for the advice and words of wisdom that I have received from my speaking event partner, Twila Le Page-Hughes. Together, we often share the stage for Conservative and patriotic style venues. She is my motivator, and this book would not be a reality without her! Please find our information on our Facebook and Twitter social media pages at The American Truth Forum. Thank you, Twila, for your love and friendship!

My dear friend, Joanie Gatley, who is a sister in my heart, you have been my role model. You made me feel strong when I was weak, and you gave me the confidence to realize that I was on a worthy and honorable path. Thank you for being my backbone and your beautiful words of wisdom!

To my bestie, Heidi Williams, who has pointed me in the direction of some very informative material for my research. I am so happy that we are in this battle for America together. We will bravely act to preserve our free nation for our children and grandchildren! One day in the distant future, I look forward to sitting in our rocking chairs with a glass of wine, a victory smile, and chatting about the time we fought for our patriotic cause and the move of God across our country!

I am so grateful to Pastor Don Strand. I truly appreciate the time and words of wisdom that you have shared with me. You are a gift to those around you!

A special thanks to my friend, who is like another brother to me, Troy Filardo. Although some of your advice was too extreme for this book (Ha! Ha! ☺), you delivered some very nice observations and words of truth. And most importantly, you gave me the guts that I needed to speak up!

I must acknowledge my teacher and mentor throughout the past five years, Lance Wallnau. You have made things so clear, and you have helped me to realize the importance of our "As One" movement to guard the soul of America. Thank you to both, you and

Annabelle, for the motivation you have given me to inspire others in the same way that you have inspired me!

Thank you to all my likeminded patriotic friends, who are in this battle with me day in and out! I love how we lift each other up and band together in our struggle to save the American Dream! Your support is a blessing to me!

May God bless you! Where We Go 1, We Go All!